Redevelopment

D0522855

by the same author

LIVING IN TRUTH
LETTERS TO OLGA

plays
LARGO DESOLATO
TEMPTATION
THREE VANĚK PLAYS

REDEVELOPMENT

or

Slum Clearance

VÁCLAV HAVEL

**English version by
James Saunders**

*from a literal translation
by Marie Winn*

WITHDRAWN

faber and faber
LONDON · BOSTON

First published in English in 1990
by Faber and Faber Limited
3 Queen Square London WC1N 3AU
Originally published by
Rowohlt Taschenbuch Verlag Gmbh
Reinbeck bei Hamburg

Phototypeset by Wilmaset Birkenhead Wirral
Printed in England by
Clays Ltd St Ives plc

All rights reserved

© Václav Havel, 1987
This translation © James Saunders, 1990

Václav Havel is hereby identified as author of this work in accordance with
Section 77 of the Copyright, Designs and Patents Act 1988.

All rights whatsoever in this play are strictly reserved and all applications to
perform it, etc. must be made in advance, before rehearsals begin, to Margaret
Ramsay, 14A Goodwin's Court, St Martin's Lane, London WC2N 4LL.

*This book is sold subject to the condition that it shall not,
by way of trade or otherwise, be lent, resold, hired out
or otherwise circulated without the publisher's prior
consent in any form of binding or cover other than that in which
it is published and without a similar condition including
this condition being imposed on the subsequent purchaser.*

A CIP record for this book is available from the British Library

ISBN 0-571-14265-6

CHARACTERS

ZDENEK BERGMAN, Principal Project Director, fifty-ish
LUISA, architect, about forty
ALBERT, architect, about twenty-five
KUZMA PLEKHANOV, architect (male)
ULCH, architect
MRS MACOURKOVA, architect
RENATA, secretary, about twenty
SPECIAL SECRETARY
FIRST INSPECTOR
SECOND INSPECTOR
FIRST DELEGATE
SECOND DELEGATE
FIRST WOMAN
SECOND WOMAN

SET

The play is set entirely in the spacious hall of a medieval castle somewhere in Czechoslovakia. Around and beneath the castle – it stands on an eminence – lies the ancient town which it once ruled. It is to prepare a plan for the redevelopment of this town that a team of architects is now quartered in the castle, their workrooms in the castle chambers.

On the right-hand side of the hall three steps lead to a massive door to the outside world (right door); along the left-hand wall is a stairway with a little balustrade which is interrupted about a yard above ground level by a landing giving access to a door in the left wall (left door). The stairway then continues to a gallery running the whole length of the rear wall, forming in effect a second floor. There are two doors giving on to the gallery (left upper door and right upper door). On the ground floor, in the rear wall beneath the gallery, are two more doors (left rear door and right rear door). There are thus six doors – one to the outside, the others to other parts of the castle.

In the centre of the hall, parallel to the front of the stage, is a great Gothic table surrounded by eight high Gothic chairs. Other chairs of various kinds, and perhaps some little tables and chests, are placed around the walls and in the corners. On the walls, together with a number of old painted portraits, are pinned architectural plans, sketches and photographs. In the middle of the central table stands a large model, in polystyrene, of a hill with a modern village at its foot and up its sides, and a Gothic castle on the summit.

Redevelopment was first performed at the Orange Tree, Richmond, on 7 September 1990, under the direction of Sam Waters.

ACT I

A violin is playing the well-known Russian song 'Ochi Cherniya'. The lights go up to reveal the player: PLEKHANOV, *alone on stage, wearing a dressing-gown and carpet slippers, his dress throughout the play. He is completely absorbed in the playing, humming spasmodically to himself. After some moments* RENATA *enters by the left door and stands on the landing waiting for him to stop. Pause.*

RENATA: Excuse me, sir.

(PLEKHANOV *doesn't hear. Pause.*)

(*Louder*) Mr Plekhanov, sir –

(PLEKHANOV *doesn't hear. Pause.*)

Excuse me, sir!

(PLEKHANOV *stops playing and looks across at her.*)

PLEKHANOV: Are you talking to me?

RENATA: The Director requests that if you must play you play something more cheerful.

(PLEKHANOV *stops playing and puts his fiddle down.* ULCH *appears at the upper right door. He wears, throughout the play, a white lab. coat.* RENATA *is leaving by the left door.*)

ULCH: Renata . . .

(RENATA *stops, hesitates for a moment, then turns to* ULCH.)

RENATA: May I help you?

ULCH: Would you have a moment?

RENATA: I'm sorry, Mr Ulch, but –

ULCH: It is important.

RENATA: I have work to do.

ULCH: We all have work to do. Please –

RENATA: I really can't just now.

(RENATA *turns quickly and goes out by the left door, leaving* ULCH *gazing after her. Pause.*)

PLEKHANOV: A mind of her own.

(ULCH *goes out through the right upper door, as* LUISA *enters by the left upper door and looks over the balustrade at* PLEKHANOV.)

LUISA: Kuzma, why aren't you playing?

(LUISA *comes slowly down the stairs.*)

PLEKHANOV: Chief doesn't like it.

LUISA: He must be having another of his bad times.

PLEKHANOV: Problems for you again, eh?

LUISA: Hm.

PLEKHANOV: Have you tried keeping him emotionally occupied?

LUISA: How do you mean?

PLEKHANOV: I don't know – pretend to be unfaithful – or jealous – suddenly overwhelm him with tenderness – or disgust . . .

(*A dog begins to bark wildly outside.* PLEKHANOV *and* LUISA *glance across at the right door. The barking stops after a moment, and there is a knock on the door.*)

LUISA: Come in!

(*Through the right door enter the* FIRST *and* SECOND DELEGATES. *The* FIRST DELEGATE *is black. They come down the steps and pause.*)

FIRST DELEGATE: Good afternoon.

SECOND DELEGATE: – noon.

(*Pause.*)

LUISA: Can I help you?

FIRST DELEGATE: We'd like to see the Project Director, please.

SECOND DELEGATE: Director, please.

LUISA: I'll see if he's free.

(LUISA *begins to mount the stairs to the left door. On the landing she stops and turns.*)

Who shall I say?

FIRST DELEGATE: We represent the citizens.

SECOND DELEGATE: –tizens.

(LUISA *and* PLEKHANOV *exchange a curious glance.*)

LUISA: Right.

(*She goes out.* PLEKHANOV *picks up his fiddle and shuffles towards the right rear door. He stops to look at them.*)

PLEKHANOV: You're looking at my dressing-gown.

FIRST DELEGATE: No no.

SECOND DELEGATE: No.

2

(PLEKHANOV *shuffles out. Pause. The* DELEGATES *look around.* ALBERT *enters by the left door and comes downstairs quickly.*)

FIRST DELEGATE: Afternoon.

SECOND DELEGATE: – noon.

ALBERT: Good afternoon.

FIRST DELEGATE: Are you the Project Director?

ALBERT: Sorry.

FIRST DELEGATE: Sorry.

SECOND DELEGATE: Sorry.

ALBERT: No no.

(ALBERT *hurries out of the left rear door. Pause. The* DELEGATES *look round.* BERGMAN *enters through the left door and walks slowly down towards the* DELEGATES.)

FIRST DELEGATE: Good afternoon.

SECOND DELEGATE: – noon.

(BERGMAN *shakes their hands, motions them to take a seat, and sits himself at the left end of the table. The* DELEGATES *remain standing. Short pause.*)

BERGMAN: What can I do for you?

FIRST DELEGATE: Are you the Project Director?

BERGMAN: Yes.

FIRST DELEGATE: We represent the two hundred and sixteen residents who signed this, erm . . .

(*He nudges the* SECOND DELEGATE, *who pulls a folded sheet of paper from his pocket.*)

SECOND DELEGATE: Signed this . . . (*Begins to read:*) 'As permanent residents of the town, we the undersigned wish to record our disapproval of the plans for redevelopment. We do not wish to live in temporary accommodation for an indefinite number of years and then return to an environment that has nothing to do with our former home. We understand that the purpose of the scheme is to improve our living conditions and health standards, but we have lived contentedly for many decades in the timeless atmosphere of this picturesque and historically unique castle town, and do not want it changed. We should be very unhappy to have our present homes taken away.'

3

FIRST DELEGATE: Signed, you see, by two hundred and sixteen citizens . . .

SECOND DELEGATE: –tizens.

(*Longer pause.*)

BERGMAN: You know, this is a serious matter . . .

FIRST DELEGATE: Oh yes.

BERGMAN: I understand your position.

FIRST DELEGATE: Good.

BERGMAN: It's only natural, from your point of view . . .

FIRST DELEGATE: We're glad you think so . . .

SECOND DELEGATE: Think so.

BERGMAN: But why are you coming to me?

FIRST DELEGATE: Well, you're in charge of the project!

BERGMAN: My dear chap, I may be in charge *here*; but it's not my brief to make judgements on the work assigned us, or change it at will. My concern is that we discharge our responsibilities as well as we can within the given parameters which –

(*He stops as the SPECIAL SECRETARY enters through the left upper door, comes quickly downstairs and approaches the SECOND DELEGATE. The SPECIAL SECRETARY walks quite noiselessly, except for one of his shoes which squeaks loudly.*)

SPECIAL SECRETARY: May I, if you please . . .?

(*He takes the paper from the SECOND DELEGATE, reads it, studies it, turns it over. Then he looks searchingly at the SECOND DELEGATE.*)

Who wrote this for you?

FIRST DELEGATE: We did . . .

SPECIAL SECRETARY: You didn't say that very convincingly.

(*Pause.*)

Well? Who then?

FIRST DELEGATE: We wrote it ourselves, really.

SECOND DELEGATE: Really.

SPECIAL SECRETARY: How do you mean, 'we'? All together? On the same pen? Is that what you mean?

FIRST DELEGATE: Everyone who signed stands behind it . . .

SPECIAL SECRETARY: I'm not asking who stands behind it or underneath it or on top of it, I'm asking who wrote it.

4

(*Pause.*)
Well, if you won't say, you won't say!
(*He walks round the table, absorbed in thought. Then he perches on the corner of the table nearest the* DELEGATES *and stares fixedly at them.*)
I understand that two thousand people live in the town. Two thousand souls, as they used to call them, crammed into small, dark, cold, damp houses with totally inadequate toilet facilities and a derisory number of baths, a source of poverty, suffering and infection. What a relic of the old social order, when the lords lived here in the castle and their subjects, their souls, down in the town. What a sad heritage. This project is not just for you, you know, it's for the good of us all!
(*Pause.*)
So?

FIRST DELEGATE: So?

SECOND DELEGATE: So?

SPECIAL SECRETARY: Will you withdraw it?

FIRST DELEGATE: We don't have the right to do that . . .

SECOND DELEGATE: The right.

SPECIAL SECRETARY: As you wish.
(*He stands up, folds the paper and pockets it, then walks round the table absorbed in thought and stops again in front of the* DELEGATES.)
How many did you say signed it?

FIRST DELEGATE: Two hundred and sixteen . . .

SECOND DELEGATE: –teen.

SPECIAL SECRETARY: About 10 per cent! And did you ask the remaining 90 per cent for their opinion?

FIRST DELEGATE: All sorts of people signed: a cross-section, different classes, different races . . . We all feel the same way . . .

SPECIAL SECRETARY: So why didn't everybody sign it? No, no, my friends, it's clear to me that these are the tactics of a pressure group, a minority pretending to speak for the majority! You won't withdraw it?

FIRST DELEGATE: No . . .

SECOND DELEGATE: No.

SPECIAL SECRETARY: Your mistake . . .

(*He turns and runs out through the left door.*)

FIRST DELEGATE: Who was that?

BERGMAN: The Special Secretary.

FIRST DELEGATE: Ah. We'd better be going . . .

BERGMAN: Just a moment . . .

FIRST DELEGATE: Yes?

BERGMAN: I don't know if this will make you feel any better, but let me say something. First: building facilities are non-existent at present, and probably will be for the foreseeable future. All we're doing is making studies. In other words, don't cross your bridges before they're built. Second: we're not barbarians. Our studies are carried out with one factor in mind: the unique spirit and needs of the particular locality we're dealing with. Why do you think we've come here and not stayed in the studio the way they usually do? We asked to be moved here so that we could breathe in the local atmosphere, get to know you, learn your preferences at first hand, your habits, your roots and ties, to wander through your winding little streets, admire your gardens, catch the scent of the rose-covered porches, peer into your wells . . . to live your kind of life, in your midst, and armed with this experience to produce something which would neither sacrifice your past nor . . . betray your future . . .

FIRST DELEGATE: Thank you.

BERGMAN: My pleasure.

(ALBERT *enters through the left rear door and hurries towards the staircase.*)

FIRST DELEGATE: We'll be off then. *Ciao.*

SECOND DELEGATE: *Ciao.*

BERGMAN: *Ciao.*

(*The* DELEGATES *exit through the right door, as* LUISA, *a cup of coffee in each hand, enters through the left door.* ALBERT *stops suddenly at the staircase and steps back to let* LUISA *past, who, as she passes, smiles at him.* ALBERT, *embarrassed, runs up the stairs and out through the left upper door.* LUISA *puts*

one coffee in front of BERGMAN *and keeps one for herself. They
sit stirring their coffees, which they will drink as they talk.
Pause.*)

LUISA: How are you feeling?

BERGMAN: I think I'm going to put an end to it.

LUISA: To what?

BERGMAN: Everything!

LUISA: Seriously, Zdenek . . .

BERGMAN: I'm dead serious.

LUISA: What's the matter?

BERGMAN: Nothing. Except that I despise myself, I hate
myself, I'm sick of myself . . .

LUISA: I get sick of myself sometimes, but that's no reason
to – !

BERGMAN: I'm so averse to life I go to bed before I'm tired and
force myself to stay asleep in the morning; at least sleep is a
kind of substitute for the non-existence I crave. Every
night before I drop off I make a wish, that I won't wake up
in the morning, that everything will be over, finished!

LUISA: You mustn't talk like that!

BERGMAN: I've become incapable of getting pleasure out of
anything, can't you see it written in the lines of my face?
My life is nothing but a tiresome duty, a source of endless
suffering. Which I then inflict on others, you above all.
What's the sense in living a life that's lost its sense?
Darkness, peace, eternal, endless, absolute peace . . .

LUISA: Stop it, that's enough! You really are a charlatan, you
know!

BERGMAN: I'm being absolutely sincere . . .

LUISA: You're only saying all this because you need someone to
pity you. Someone to console you, flatter you, worry about
you; despair over you. It's just attention-seeking: you're
trying to involve other people in your problems so as to
find a kind of self-justification in their anxiety, some
external proof that you actually exist. The fact is, you
exploit everybody around you! You're like a spoilt child!
(*Pause.*)

BERGMAN: Luisa . . .

7

LUISA: What?

BERGMAN: A beautiful woman like you, desirable, good-hearted
– you could easily find someone else to be happy with.
Someone you admired. Why don't you?

LUISA: You see! That's what I mean!

BERGMAN: What is?

LUISA: Just what I'm talking about! You said that purely and
simply to get me to fall on my knees and cry through my
tears that I can't live without you!

BERGMAN: You think that's what I'm after? Cheap melodrama?

LUISA: You'd love it! The cheaper the better!

BERGMAN: Luisa, if your Freudian interpretations explained my
condition I'd be only too happy. But it's deeper than that.
It's not a psychological problem! It's metaphysical! I don't
need self-justification, I need meaning! But of course you
love that kind of simple diagnosis; then you can write out a
simple prescription: take no notice and it'll go away!
(*Pause.*)
(*Quietly*) Luisa . . .

LUISA: Hm?

BERGMAN: Don't you at least feel now and then . . . just a tiny
bit sorry for me?

LUISA: Now and then . . . a tiny bit.

BERGMAN: Luisa . . .

LUISA: Come to me then . . . There, there . . . There,
there . . .
(BERGMAN *sinks to his knees in front of* LUISA, *embracing her,
pressing his head to her lap.* LUISA *strokes his head pensively.*
RENATA *enters by the left door. On the landing she stops, looks
down as if she wants to speak but, seeing* BERGMAN *at*
LUISA's *feet, decides to leave. However,* ULCH *has appeared at
the right upper door.*)

ULCH: Renata . . .
(RENATA *stops, hesitates, then turns to* ULCH. *At the sound of*
ULCH's *voice* BERGMAN *gets up quickly and returns to
normal.*)

RENATA: May I help you?

ULCH: Would you have a moment?

8

RENATA: I have work to do, Mr Ulch –

ULCH: We all have work to do. Please . . .

RENATA: I really can't just now.

(RENATA *goes out quickly by the left door.* ULCH's *eyes follow her.* PLEKHANOV *appears, carrying his fiddle, at the right rear door. He stands in the doorway, and begins to play softly a lyrical tune.*)

ULCH: A mind of her own!

(*The lights go down, but the music continues through the intermission.*)

ACT II

The stage is empty, but the music may still be heard playing; but it presently stops, as RENATA *and* LUISA *enter by the left rear door.* RENATA *is carrying seven plates,* LUISA *has napkins and tableware. They go to the table and begin to lay it.*

RENATA: So you think it's all right, Luisa?

LUISA: It depends on the circumstances. For instance, you're less likely to do it with someone if you're in love with someone else than if you're on your own, or in a long-term relationship. And obviously it's easier with someone who attracts you than with someone you find revolting. Then you have to take into account your moral values and how strong they are, whether it's momentary lust or a matter of life and death, and so on. It's complicated . . .

RENATA: I couldn't do it with someone I didn't love!

LUISA: Don't be too sure! Still, I hope so for your sake! You'll have fewer problems that way . . .

RENATA: We've laid one too many again.

LUISA: You, me, Ulch, Plekhanov, Albert, Bergman . . . Mrs Macourkova.

RENATA: I always forget Mrs Macourkova.

(RENATA *and* LUISA *finish laying the table and go out through the left rear door.* ULCH *appears at the right upper door, sees nobody, and disappears again.* RENATA *and* LUISA *enter through the left rear door,* RENATA *with several bottles of beer,* LUISA *carrying a tray of glasses and bottle openers. These they lay out on the table.*)

Is it true that if two people do it who don't love each other, she's more likely to fall in love with him afterwards than he is with her?

LUISA: Well, you know, a woman looks for stability, something solid and permanent; her sights tend to be set on home and family, so any liaison is seen as a possible relationship . . .

RENATA: I'm not sure I could do it even with someone I *was* in love with.

LUISA: How gorgeously innocent you are! Don't worry, Renata, when you're really in love it'll happen and you won't even know how. All at once it will seem so obvious, so simple, so natural and so pure . . .

(They finish laying the table and go out by the left rear door. ULCH appears at the right rear door, sees nobody and disappears again. RENATA and LUISA enter through the left rear door, RENATA with a pot of goulash and a ladle, LUISA with a basket of rolls.)

(Calls out) Dinner!

(They set down the pot and the basket; RENATA passes LUISA the plates, into which LUISA ladles the goulash. Meanwhile the others enter: ULCH from the right upper door, then PLEKHANOV with his fiddle through the right rear door; then ALBERT through the left rear door, and finally BERGMAN through the left door. BERGMAN sits in his chair at the left end of the table, after which the others sit down. RENATA opens the bottles and pours beer for the others; then she and LUISA sit down. A pause: they look towards BERGMAN, who is far away. He comes to himself, realizing that the others are waiting for him.)

BERGMAN: Sorry . . . Well – *bon appetit!*

ALL: *Bon appetit!*

(They begin to eat. Pause. MACOURKOVA enters by the left rear door and hurries to her seat.)

MACOURKOVA: I'm so sorry . . .

(She sits down quickly and begins to eat. Pause.)

PLEKHANOV: Do you know there's an interesting legend about this castle? I discovered it today in the library . . .

LUISA: A ghost story, I hope.

PLEKHANOV: A certain countess, the wife of an ancient lord of the castle, fell madly in love with her groom . . .

LUISA: Oh, a love story . . .

PLEKHANOV: Listen. As a result, they say, the count's ghost wreaks his revenge on any man in love who enters his walls . . .

LUISA: How does he do that?

PLEKHANOV: By throwing him off the tower, into the moat.

ULCH: Every castle has its legends. I've heard better.

PLEKHANOV: The last count was in fact found dead in the moat; the older people down there still remember it. Though since it happened the day before he had his marching orders, other explanations do present themselves.

ULCH: When we convert the moat to a swimming pool it'll put a damper on that story.

PLEKHANOV: I take these legends with a pinch of salt, but I must admit I sense in the tower a certain – ambience.

LUISA: You spend your life sensing ambiences, Kuzma. Stop trying to scare us!

ULCH: I have an idea! For that two-storey building in Zone Two of the Public Utilities! Next to the Children's Play Area! A permanent exhibition on superstition and prejudice! To gently indoctrinate children into the scientific approach so that –

(*He stops. The* SPECIAL SECRETARY *enters by the right upper door, crosses the gallery and descends the stairs.*)

MACOURKOVA: Good evening, Secretary!

SPECIAL SECRETARY: Good evening, Mrs –

MACOURKOVA: Macourkova. Why don't you ever dine with us? It would be jolly!

SPECIAL SECRETARY: Do you think so?

(*He crosses to the right door and goes out. Pause.*)

PLEKHANOV: Why is it, do you think, that only one of the Special Secretary's shoes squeaks?

(*A slightly embarrassed titter.*)

ALBERT: What did the men want?

BERGMAN: Hm? What men?

ALBERT: The men from down there.

BERGMAN: Oh, they're opposed to the redevelopment. They think we want to take their homes away.

ULCH: Typical of those people! If we took their attitude into account nothing would ever be built! Civilization would become moribund!

(*Slight pause.*)

ALBERT: What did you tell them?

BERGMAN: What could *I* tell them? The Special Secretary had a word with them. He called it the tactics of a pressure group.

(*Slight pause.*)

ULCH: If you ask me we're being cackhanded about the whole thing.

BERGMAN: Cackhanded about what?

ULCH: Hidden away up here, making our plans, nobody knows what they are . . . Naturally they get wild ideas . . .

BERGMAN: And how do you think we *should* go about it? Run down and get their approval for every sketch we do?

ULCH: No no. But for instance, if we organized a series of popular lectures to explain to them, in terms they could understand, how much nicer it'll be once they've got central heating, a decent House of Culture, a Central Laundry, Refuse Disposal . . . they'd begin to see that our sole aim is to enhance the quality of their lives. I dare say most of them haven't the faintest idea they're still living in the last century!

ALBERT: I'm sorry – !

ULCH: You disagree? I thought you'd like the idea.

ALBERT: I'm sorry, but you're making those people out to be stupid. Do you think they've never seen a modern housing project?

ULCH: I dare say they have, but all they see –

ALBERT: And you're surprised that we terrify them? I'd be surprised if we didn't!

ULCH: Albert, I realize that some uninformed laymen like to write off the whole of modern architecture on the basis of one or two less-than-perfect examples, which I admit do exist, but as far as I know you are a qualified architect –

LUISA: He didn't say he agrees with them. Only that he's not surprised at them.

ULCH: I don't see the difference!

ALBERT: Look, I'm not against new buildings *per se* –

ULCH: Then what are you saying? That we should use medieval methods to build them?

ALBERT: We couldn't if we tried. We wouldn't know how.

ULCH: Who needs to? Things have changed, Albert, since your grandfather's time. And I'm not just talking about prefabrication and synthetic materials –

ALBERT: What then? What's changed?

ULCH: Good Lord, what did you do at college, Albert? Generations of the finest architectural minds have spent their genius on the concept of the city of the future; we're the cutting edge of all that. We know how to design the ideal living environment, aesthetically pleasing but structurally coherent, a smoothly running complex of efficient communication systems, state-of-the-art commercial networks, parks, rest areas and entertainment zones. And you think we should leave them to live in holes in the ground for the sake of a feudal past!

ALBERT: It's what they tried to teach me at college that makes me understand those people down there!

ULCH: Elucidate, Albert, elucidate.

ALBERT: What they know better than us down there is how complicated things can get in your ideal city. It needs more than planning!

ULCH: So in your opinion urban renewal is bunkum –

ALBERT: I'm not saying that! I'm saying that cities worth living in are like part of nature, they need to develop over the centuries, they're the result of – how can I explain it? – generations of experience, quietly collected and handed down – people's feelings, evolving historically, anonymous people, people with a sense of humility in the face of everything that seems beyond their understanding, their . . .

ULCH: In the face of what? Can you be specific?

ALBERT: I'm talking about their respect for the character of the countryside, the laws of nature, the legacy their ancestors left them, that beauty of form that comes of different kinds of people living together over a long period of –

ULCH: But, bloody hell, we –

PLEKHANOV: Please! Let him finish what he's saying. (*To* ALBERT) Do go on.

14

ALBERT: I've finished. I'm only worried at the idea of sweeping everything away like a load of old rubbish and replacing it with a mental concept. None of us has a formula for universal happiness, and we have no right to overturn people's lives as if we had . . .

ULCH: Who was it suggested organizing lectures and discussion groups?

ALBERT: What's the good of discussions when you've already decided you're right and they're wrong? You may feel superior, I don't! Not when I think of that hideous housing project out there, you know the one, they do anyway; ruined countryside all round. You say 'less than perfect', as if that kind of thing is a sort of oversight. It's not, it's the logical end product of the conceit of architects who think they understand how life works. If you want an example of your ideal living environment why not be honest and use a battery chicken farm!

ULCH: Coffee-house philosophy. Very trendy, Albert, but like most trendy ideas not very original. Every conservative reactionary in the country spouts that stuff, it's their stock in trade. Return to the past, respect tradition, etc., etc. Forget about scientific and technological progress, pretend micro-electronics and space rockets don't exist. We live in a global civilization, Albert, with all the enormous problems that come with it, not least the population explosion; and you want us to abandon everything and leave the world to its fate!

ALBERT: You can't solve everything in your mind! That's all I'm saying. You can't. If you want proof, look at this modern world you're so fond of. We're laying it waste in the name of progress! We're not improving life, we're manipulating it to death!

ULCH: Oh, bravo!

ALBERT: I don't think it's a laughing matter.

ULCH: I'm sorry. So what do you recommend?

ALBERT: It's obvious, isn't it? Adaptability – humility – respect for human standards, for life at its own level – respect for

its diversity, its unpredictability, its mystery . . .
Respect . . .

(*A short, rather embarrassed pause. Then they all turn to*
BERGMAN.)

BERGMAN: May I break in here? I'm glad to hear the various
viewpoints expressed so sharply and – forcefully. It makes
for a lively debate, and that can lead to something.
Personally, I found what was said most useful: it makes me
realize with renewed urgency the purpose of our mission
here: not to force on the people our private utopias – which
luckily we have no capacity to carry out at present; neither,
though, to abandon our expertise and rely on tradition and
the spontaneous creativity of the anonymous masses to
solve today's complex problems of urban existence for us.
The only way left, then, is to seek out with incisiveness but
sensitivity such architectonic solutions as may be in
harmony with the tasks, demands and possibilities of the
time, and with the natural and basically unpredictable
diversity of life. In other words, I'm for progress, Ulch;
but progress, Albert, with a human face. (*To*
MACOURKOVA) What is your opinion on this, Mrs
Macourkova?

MACOURKOVA: Oh, well, you know . . .

(*She shrugs her shoulders uncertainly.*)

BERGMAN: Yes . . .

(*He gets up, nods slightly to the others and leaves, up the stairs
to the left door. The others also get up. While* RENATA *and*
LUISA *begin to clear the table* ULCH *goes upstairs to the
gallery. Picking up his fiddle,* PLEKHANOV *strums a chord on
it, and slaps* ALBERT *enthusiastically on the back.*)

PLEKHANOV: Good, Albert! Very good!

(ALBERT, *whose eyes were on* LUISA, *is embarrassed.*
PLEKHANOV *goes out by the right rear door as the* SPECIAL
SECRETARY *comes in by the left rear door, and makes for the
stairs.*)

MACOURKOVA: Secretary!

SPECIAL SECRETARY: Mrs . . .

MACOURKOVA: Macourkova! You seem so busy; I hope you're sleeping well!

SPECIAL SECRETARY: Very well. Good night.

MACOURKOVA: Sweet dreams!

(*The* SPECIAL SECRETARY *nods, goes downstairs to the left door and exits.* RENATA *and* LUISA *leave by the left rear door carrying some of the dishes, etc.* MACOURKOVA *follows them out through the same door.* ULCH, *on the gallery, looks down at* ALBERT.)

ULCH: Given your views, I wonder you ever joined this profession.

ALBERT: When there's a threat to life, someone's got to protect it!

ULCH: You're not protecting life. You're protecting never-never land. Good night.

(ULCH *goes out by the left upper door.* RENATA *and* LUISA *come in again by the left rear door.* RENATA *glances across at* ALBERT, *who is, however, gazing at* LUISA. RENATA *and* LUISA *clear the rest of the table.*)

ALBERT: Do you need any help?

LUISA: Thanks, Albert, we can manage.

(RENATA *and* LUISA *go out by the left rear door with the remainder of the dishes, as the* SPECIAL SECRETARY *enters by the left upper door. Coming downstairs, he walks towards the right rear door.*)

ALBERT: Secretary!

SPECIAL SECRETARY: (*Stopping*) What is it?

ALBERT: Where are they?

SPECIAL SECRETARY: Who?

ALBERT: Those people's representatives . . .

SPECIAL SECRETARY: Why does that interest you?

ALBERT: No particular reason . . .

SPECIAL SECRETARY: They're in custody.

ALBERT: You mean in the dungeon?

SPECIAL SECRETARY: Don't worry, they're not hungry there. But since you've mentioned it, I've a question for you.

ALBERT: Which is?

SPECIAL SECRETARY: You don't happen to know who wrote the petition for them?

ALBERT: No, why should I?

SPECIAL SECRETARY: Are you sure? Do try to remember.

ALBERT: I've told you, I don't know!

SPECIAL SECRETARY: Well, we shall see . . .

(*He squeaks out by the right rear door.* ALBERT, *thinking deeply, crosses to a chair and flops down in it.* RENATA *and* LUISA *come in by the left rear door.*)

LUISA: Good night then, Renata. Thanks for your help.

RENATA: Good night.

(RENATA *goes upstairs to the left door, but stops on the landing to glance at* ALBERT. *He doesn't notice, so she goes out by the left door.* LUISA *goes up to* ALBERT, *strokes his head and sits down beside him.*)

LUISA: That was quite a show you put on, Albert.

ALBERT: I let myself get carried away, it was stupid . . .

LUISA: It's good to hear *someone* around here saying what they feel.

ALBERT: Do you think there'll be trouble?

LUISA: Zdenek will fix it; I'll tell him.

ALBERT: Thank you.

(*Pause.*)

LUISA: I rather envy you . . .

ALBERT: Me? For goodness' sake, why?

LUISA: Your youth . . .

ALBERT: You talk as if you're old!

LUISA: I only mean you haven't been spoiled by the world yet; unlike the rest of us.

ALBERT: Not you!

LUISA: I'm not sure about that. I used to make speeches like that once upon a time. We all did . . .

ALBERT: Even Ulch?

LUISA: Even Ulch. His kind of speech, of course. But at least with real passion.

(*Pause.*)

ALBERT: I don't know what to do . . .

LUISA: Be yourself.

ALBERT: Whoever that is . . . Everything seems unreal to me –
this castle, the project, everyone here – I know exactly
what they're going to say, what they're going to do – It's as
if they're not people but characters in a play someone's
putting on –

LUISA: When life teaches *you* to be cautious, Albert, you'll also
learn to be more careful how you judge the rest of us . . .
Oh, forget I said that. You're quite right.

ALBERT: I wasn't including you!

LUISA: Why ever not?

ALBERT: You're different. There's something special about you
– if I got into trouble you'd be the one I'd come to . . .

LUISA: Like a mother?

ALBERT: God, no, I'm sorry, I didn't mean it like that!

LUISA: No need to apologize.

(*Pause.*)

ALBERT: They've put them in the dungeon! It's grotesque . . .

LUISA: Par for the course.

ALBERT: Can't something be done?

LUISA: I'll ask Zdenek.

(PLEKHANOV *appears at the right rear door, tuning his fiddle,
holding it to his ear. Neither* LUISA *nor* ALBERT *sees him.*
LUISA *stands up; then* ALBERT *also stands.*)

Don't look so agonized. Go to bed. Forget it. Here, come
here.

(*She kisses him on the forehead.*)

There. A motherly kiss goodnight.

(ALBERT *hesitates, then backs away in confusion towards the
left rear door.* LUISA, *smiling at him, waves; he waves back
awkwardly, and backs out of the left rear door as* PLEKHANOV
begins to play a lyrical tune. LUISA *looks up at him.*)

A nice lad, isn't he?

PLEKHANOV: Oh yes . . . He's in love with you.

LUISA: Do you think so?

PLEKHANOV: I'm never wrong about these things . . .

(*He begins to play more loudly as the lights go down.*)

ACT III

PLEKHANOV, *who has played throughout the intermission, is on stage with* ALBERT. *He plays for a few moments longer, then puts the fiddle down. Pause.*

ALBERT: Imagine, for instance, you've a momentous decision to make, two choices, A or B. You know choice A would be in your interest, but at the same time a certain voice tells you that the right thing to do is B –
(RENATA *enters by the left door, carrying a tray with two cups of coffee on it. She begins to climb the stairs but, hearing what* ALBERT *is saying, she stops and listens attentively.*)
It's only a voice in your own head, yet you have the feeling that *it*'s in charge of you, it seems to matter in some mysterious way. You want to do what it tells you; and even though you finally decide to do the other thing you at least try to explain why, defend yourself in front of it, get its approval. You must know what I'm talking about!
(RENATA *goes quickly out by the left upper door.* ULCH *looks out from the right upper door, just fails to see* RENATA, *and disappears again.*)
PLEKHANOV: Yes, go on. What about it?
ALBERT: Well, that mysterious inner voice – what can it be but the voice of the Supreme Being?
PLEKHANOV: I think it's a little more complicated than that, my friend –
(RENATA, *her tray empty, enters by the left upper door and descends the stairs. At the landing she stops again and listens.*)
ALBERT: Yes, I know I'm oversimplifying, but even so – I mean how would we know a thing was good if there weren't some kind of standard outside us? Our sense of goodness doesn't just come from ourselves. It's a sense of harmony with something that was here before us and will be here after us, something eternal. That's what I think. A harmony that

makes us – insignificant. I don't know how to talk about these things, but it seems so obvious to me . . .

RENATA: Oh, and to me! . . . Sorry!

(*She runs through the left door in confusion.* ALBERT *watches this in surprise. Slight pause.*)

PLEKHANOV: She's in love with you.

ALBERT: With me? Nonsense!

PLEKHANOV: I'm never wrong about these things. But to get back to your little sermon: for most of us, I'm afraid, that voice you talk about is no more than a faint dying whisper nowadays; hum a little tune to yourself and you drown it out completely. Yours won't make your life any easier, but I hope it lasts. Because I'll tell you this for what it's worth, Albert: the persistence of your inner voice may be the only thing keeping a certain fiddle-playing eccentric from the absolute conviction that everything is definitively and finally up shit creek.

(*He plucks a single disharmonious chord on his fiddle, pats* ALBERT *gently on the back and goes out by the right rear door, leaving* ALBERT *to ponder on this.* BERGMAN *and* LUISA *come in by the left door and come downstairs.*)

BERGMAN: Greetings, Albert. Ça va?

ALBERT: Good morning. Look, I, erm . . .

BERGMAN: Cooled down a little this morning?

ALBERT: I'm sorry about yesterday. I was – a little . . .

BERGMAN: No need for apologies, I'm not angry. But a word of friendly advice: it really would be advisable to express yourself a little more circumspectly, at least in front of some of our colleagues. There's nothing that can't be said, of course, we need the occasional gust of fresh air blowing through; but a little more strategy might better serve the interests of your cause, as well as your own. I'm sure you understand me.

ALBERT: Yes . . . Yes, of course . . .

(*A short embarrassed pause;* ALBERT *glances across at* LUISA, *who smiles at him.*)

Well, I'll erm . . .

(*He exits by the left rear door.* BERGMAN *and* LUISA *sit down.*)

BERGMAN: We're going to have complications over him . . .

LUISA: I'm sure you can fix things.

BERGMAN: Save his job, you mean?

LUISA: If that's what it comes to.

BERGMAN: Bergman the fixer. Sorting out, defending, explaining, manoeuvring. Not even any gratitude, they despise me for it! How I'd love to change places with that boy! To say any damned thing I like knowing there's always some ageing idiot to pull me out of it – wouldn't that be marvellous!

LUISA: You should be glad to have someone like him around.

BERGMAN: You're fond of him, aren't you?

LUISA: At least he's a real person.

BERGMAN: Unlike me? . . . Good-looking too.

LUISA: Yes, that too.

BERGMAN: Yes. Well, it's understandable for a woman of your age to want to dispense her bounty in that direction.

LUISA: And I suppose it's understandable for a man of your age to see everything in the crudest terms.

(*Pause.*)

How are you feeling?

BERGMAN: In one sense, better.

LUISA: In what sense?

BERGMAN: I went up to the tower this morning.

LUISA: What for? Meditation?

BERGMAN: Yes. With that legend of Plekhanov's in my mind. I stood there for ages looking down at the moat . . .

LUISA: And did you find enlightenment?

BERGMAN: Oh yes. I realized that it would be quick and easy. And very possible . . .

(*The* SPECIAL SECRETARY *enters by the right upper door, crosses the gallery quickly, runs down to the left door and goes out. Slight pause.*)

LUISA: Will you speak to him about those men?

BERGMAN: What men?

LUISA: Those two in the dungeon.

22

BERGMAN: I will at the right moment. He's obviously taken up
with something just now.
(*Pause.*)
You're not interested.
LUISA: In what?
BERGMAN: I was talking about the tower.
LUISA: Oh, that. You know, I've been thinking over what you
said yesterday . . .
BERGMAN: And what conclusion did you reach?
LUISA: That it *is* more complicated than I thought . . .
BERGMAN: Ah!
LUISA: I don't know about its being metaphysical, but it's
certainly not just psychological. I'd call it existential. Here
you are, playing the role of the wise man guarding our
studio from the turmoil of the world, and not making a bad
job of it; at the same time, deep inside, you suspect that
this role is nothing but fancy dress, behind which hides a
rather ordinary conformist thrashing about in a rather
ordinary way. And of course this doubt about the reality of
your role includes a doubt about your own identity, even
your very existence: if your grand mission is merely an
illusion, the terrifying thought must have struck you that
the illusion extends to your very self.
(*The* SPECIAL SECRETARY *enters by the right rear door,
hurries across the room, runs up the staircase and out by the left
upper door.*)
Such thoughts must be hard to live with. So you look for a
way out, a way to convince yourself that you actually exist
as a real person. It's not to be found in your public life, so
you look to the private one. In other words, you use your
anxieties, depressions, death wishes, to demonstrate at
every moment that you are a man and not a fiction; your
obsession with non-existence proves your existence, your
preoccupation with death proves you're still alive . . .
(*The* SPECIAL SECRETARY *enters by the left door and runs
down towards the right rear door.*)
BERGMAN: Is something going on?
SPECIAL SECRETARY: Not for the moment . . .

(*He goes out by the right rear door.*)

LUISA: The trouble is of course that it's all a fake, all a substitute. Your posturings about private pressures cover your lack of public courage. So in fact you commit a further fraud on yourself, escaping from one illusion into another, robbing Peter to pay Paul. Sooner or later you'll realize this, see that you're nothing but illusions, substitutions and borrowings, that there are no more Peters to rob. Only *then* will you be seized by a real despair and a real wish to die. And only then will I seriously begin to fear for you . . .

(*Slight pause. Then* BERGMAN *suddenly begins to sob like a child. For a moment* LUISA *looks at him in surprise; then she goes up to him and begins gently to kiss the tears from his eyes.*) There there . . . No, stop it, I didn't mean to hurt you . . . I was only trying to help . . .

(*The* SPECIAL SECRETARY *enters by the left rear door.* LUISA *draws away from* BERGMAN, *who tries to return to normal.*)

SPECIAL SECRETARY: Are all your people in the building?

BERGMAN: Yes. Why?

SPECIAL SECRETARY: Call them together, please, at once.

BERGMAN: Is something going on?

SPECIAL SECRETARY: You'll see soon enough.

(*He goes out by the right door, leaving it open as he goes.*
BERGMAN *goes to the stairs and calls out towards the left door.*)

BERGMAN: Renata!

LUISA: Wipe your eyes.

(RENATA *enters by the left door and stands on the landing.*)

BERGMAN: Call everybody, will you?

RENATA: Now?

BERGMAN: Yes, now!

(RENATA *runs downstairs towards the left rear door as* ULCH *enters on to the gallery from the right upper door.*)

ULCH: Renata, I must talk to you!

RENATA: There's no time now, we have a meeting.

ULCH: After the meeting then . . .

(*But* RENATA *has gone out by the left rear door.* ULCH *comes downstairs slowly.* ALBERT *enters by the left rear door, followed by* RENATA, *who makes straight for the right rear door and out. A dog begins to bark wildly outside; everybody stops and looks towards the right door.* RENATA *comes in through the right rear door, followed by* PLEKHANOV *carrying his violin, which he deposits carefully, looking towards the right door, as does* RENATA. *The barking stops. A slight pause, as they wait in suspense.*)

SPECIAL SECRETARY: (*Offstage*) Hallo!

FIRST INSPECTOR: (*Offstage*) *Ciao!* Are they ready for me, Mishak?

SPECIAL SECRETARY: (*Offstage*) All ready.

(MACOURKOVA *runs in panting by the left rear door. After a slight pause the* FIRST INSPECTOR *enters by the right door. He is black. The* SPECIAL SECRETARY *follows him, closing the door after him. They stop on the stairs. The others watch, confused, but the* FIRST INSPECTOR *gazes round with a smile.*)

FIRST INSPECTOR: *Ciao!*

BERGMAN: (*Uncertainly*) *Ciao . . .*

SPECIAL SECRETARY: It's my pleasant duty to introduce our new Inspector of Projects, his predecessor having gone into well-deserved retirement. Our friend here wishes to say a few words about his views on the project . . .

FIRST INSPECTOR: Sit down, please, make yourselves comfortable.

(*Bewildered, they all sit down round the table. The* FIRST INSPECTOR *sits on the stairs by the right door, the* SPECIAL SECRETARY *sitting next to him.*)

Right, now, you're all expecting a long boring speech. Well, you're not getting one. We've all had our bellyful of bullshit, right?

(*Nervous laughter.*)

That's the first thing. Second: let's not be *afraid* of each other. We're all in the same boat, right? Which at the moment is paddling backwards up shit creek, right?

(*Nervous laughter.* PLEKHANOV *in particular gives an incredulous laugh, twanging his fiddle.*)

MACOURKOVA: Excuse me, Inspector –

FIRST INSPECTOR: Miss –

MACOURKOVA: Macourkova, Mrs Macourkova. I wondered if
you'd care for a cup of coffee?

FIRST INSPECTOR: No offence, Mrs M., but I had a cup of the
real thing this morning, special issue, know what I mean?
(*Polite laughter.*)
Now, I may be the new boy, right, but I'm not stupid. I
sussed out this situation p.d. bloody q. Some thickhead at
the top tells you what to do, right? And you say, yes sir, no
sir, three bags full, sir. Get out of order and you're im
shtook, am I right?
(*They nod in bewilderment.*)
Friends, those days are over. Put it this way, you're ace
architects, you don't want a bunch of know-nothing
dickheads talking out of their arses at you from Mount
Olympus, pardon my Polish. Let's face it, this whole
project was a pig's ear from day one, you know it, I know
it, even they know it down there. Now don't get me wrong;
better pads with plumbing, sewerage, and all mod. cons,
no one's arguing. But bulldozing the lot and shoving up
highrises? Forget it. That's the simple way, yes, so was
Dresden. But it offends your susceptibilities because it's
bloody outrageous, am I right?
(*They nod in bewilderment.*)
What they don't dig up there is that people are individuals,
they want to do their own thing, know what I mean?
Here's a pigeon-fancier, there's a rabbit-man, why not if
that's their bag? This was my manor, friends, I was
dragged up here so I know what I'm talking about. But to
get to the nitty-gritty: bulldozing is out, right. So what's
in, you ask? How the fuck should we know, excuse my
Estonian? You're the experts, you tell us, it's your ball-
game. Use your expertise, focus those fine-tuned brains on
the problem and come up with something fantastic! Not for
here, maybe, don't feel tied down, if you get some fab
notion that won't work here, it might work somewhere else
and we can do a swap. Know what I mean?
(*A short embarrassed pause.*)

BERGMAN: I think I speak not only for myself but for all my
   colleagues when I –
FIRST INSPECTOR: You are – excuse me?
BERGMAN: Zdenek Bergman. I'm the Project Director.
FIRST INSPECTOR: So you're in charge here?
BERGMAN: Only if you want me to be, I mean . . .
FIRST INSPECTOR: It's not what I want, friend. They're the
   ones! (*To the others*) You reckon this fella?
   (*They nod.*)
   Fair enough, you got the job. Only cut the crap, keep it
   short, know what I mean?
BERGMAN: Yes. I think I speak for all of us in saying that we've
   waited years for this moment. By its nature, you see,
   architecture desperately needs freedom –
FIRST INSPECTOR: Well, there you go! You're on your own.
   Any hassle, just give me a bell. Better still, tell Mishak
   here, *he*'ll give me a bell. What are Special Secretaries for?
   So –
   (*The* FIRST INSPECTOR *gets up, followed by the* SPECIAL
   SECRETARY *and then everyone else.*)
   So good luck! Good luck!
ALBERT: Inspector . . .
FIRST INSPECTOR: Uhuh?
ALBERT: I don't know whether you know, but some time ago
   when we were still at the planning stage, two of the
   townspeople brought up a petition criticizing the scheme.
   The result was that they were interned in the dungeon.
   Couldn't this injustice be put right?
FIRST INSPECTOR: Let them out, Mishak!
SPECIAL SECRETARY: Both of them?
FIRST INSPECTOR: Both of them, yes! So, friends – *Ciao!*
ALL: *Ciao!*
   (*The* FIRST INSPECTOR *waves and leaves, by the right door,
   with the* SPECIAL SECRETARY. *A stunned silence as they all
   stare at the right door.*)
ALBERT: Freedom!
   (*The others come to themselves; saying 'Freedom', embracing
   each other.*)

27

PLEKHANOV: I've seen some changes in my time, but I never dreamed the likes of this. Did you, Zdenek?

BERGMAN: Oh, I dreamed it . . .

LUISA: Maybe it *is* a dream.

ALBERT: No! *That* was the dream! It had to happen – we've woken up! We're alive again!

PLEKHANOV: For as long as it lasts . . .

BERGMAN: It's got to last!

ALBERT: No more excuses for us now!

BERGMAN: Once in a lifetime! It's got to last!

(*They subside slowly; some of them sit at the table.* RENATA *stands to one side. Slight pause.*)

ULCH: I don't wish to be a wet blanket . . .

LUISA: Ulch, you're not going to carp at this as well.

ULCH: No, of course I'm delighted. I'm only afraid we may be in danger of throwing the baby out with the bathwater . . .

BERGMAN: What are you talking about, Ulch?

ULCH: I only want to point out that to break free from incompetent management is one thing; to throw overboard all rational thinking on town planning is something else . . .

LUISA: Who's talking about throwing anything overboard?

ULCH: Nobody yet; but I foresee moves in that direction. Personally, I have to make my position clear: I refuse to subscribe to any attempt to take urban architectonics back to the primitive, chaotic and antisocial forms of the last century –

BERGMAN: None of us wants that, Ulch! You're crying doom unnecessarily, my friend.

ULCH: Maybe so, but the point had to be made. As I see it, it's essential that our dislike of centralism doesn't degenerate into a dislike of conceptualization in general . . .

PLEKHANOV: You talk as if there are only two possibilities: bureaucratic control or anarchy –

ALBERT: Exactly! To promote pluralism instead of uniformism isn't to choose chaos instead of order but life instead of death!

ULCH: I've nothing against pluralism! Just to remind you that freedom doesn't mean irresponsibility!

BERGMAN: Absolutely! As I see it, freedom means not irresponsibility but a golden chance to finally fulfil our creative responsibility! It's primarily a moral question: we must put truth above lies, courage above conformity, freedom above repression. The braver we are as people, the better we'll be as architects. Let's be honest: we've spent years designing bad buildings. Why? I'll tell you: because we were never given our heads! Of course some of us will think globally, others individualistically. The main thing is that we do what we want to do, not what we are forced to do. Our projects must be born in an atmosphere of free discussion, mutual tolerance, Ulch, good will and efficient collaboration. To create and defend such an atmosphere is the task we must now set ourselves.

PLEKHANOV: No more taboos.

ALBERT: Fear must give way to truth!

BERGMAN: Obedience must give way to responsibility!

LUISA: Stupidity must give way to freedom!

BERGMAN: What is your opinion about all this, Mrs Macourkova?

(MACOURKOVA *shrugs her shoulders indecisively*.)

MACOURKOVA: Oh well, you know . . .

(*Slight pause.*)

BERGMAN: Yes . . .

LUISA: Is this a good time for the celebration bubbly?

BERGMAN: What better?

(LUISA *gestures to* RENATA, *and they go out by the left rear door. As they do so, the* SPECIAL SECRETARY *comes through the right rear door, with the* TWO DELEGATES.)

PLEKHANOV: 'And the graves shall open . . .'

BERGMAN: Welcome to freedom, my friend. Didn't I tell you not to worry? And have no fears about your town, we shan't ruin it.

FIRST DELEGATE: Thank you.

BERGMAN: No no, the thanks are ours. We see now that we

have a common cause; we fight together. Our greetings to the town! *Ciao*!

FIRST DELEGATE: *Ciao*.

SECOND DELEGATE: *Ciao*.

(*They go towards the right door with the* SPECIAL SECRETARY.)

MACOURKOVA: Secretary . . .

SPECIAL SECRETARY: Yes?

MACOURKOVA: Won't you stay for a little drink with us? We're celebrating.

SPECIAL SECRETARY: I never drink. *Ciao* . . .

MACOURKOVA: *Ciao*.

(*The* SPECIAL SECRETARY *goes out by the right door, as* LUISA *and* RENATA *enter by the left rear door,* LUISA *with a tray of glasses,* RENATA *with four bottles of champagne.* LUISA *passes out the glasses,* BERGMAN *and* PLEKHANOV *take two of the bottles, while* RENATA *puts the other two on the table.* BERGMAN *and* PLEKHANOV *open the bottles with a pop and fill the glasses.*)

RENATA: Real champagne!

LUISA: Or almost!

BERGMAN: (*Raising his glass*) Colleagues! I give you a toast! To the unfettered advance of architecture! To urbanism with a human face!

ALL: (*Clinking glasses*) Urbanism with a human face!

(*They drink.* BERGMAN *and* PLEKHANOV *refill their glasses.*)

PLEKHANOV: (*Raising his glass*) I drink to the end of official vandalism!

ALL: (*Clinking glasses*) Hurray!

LUISA: (*Raising her glass*) I drink to the death of fear!

ALL: (*Clinking glasses*) Hurray!

PLEKHANOV: *Now* I can play a jolly tune!

(*He seizes his fiddle and begins to play the 'Blue Danube' waltz.*)

LUISA: And now we can dance!

(BERGMAN *takes* LUISA, *and begins to dance.*)

BERGMAN: Why aren't you dancing? You are all to dance! That's an order!

ALBERT: No more orders!

ULCH: Down with orders! But everyone must dance!

(ULCH *grabs* RENATA, ALBERT *takes* MACOURKOVA *and they begin to dance. After a while they change partners:* BERGMAN *dances with* MACOURKOVA, ULCH *with* LUISA, ALBERT *with* RENATA. PLEKHANOV *speeds up the tempo, they grow wilder in their dancing. After a while the men again change partners:* BERGMAN *is now with* RENATA, ULCH *with* MACOURKOVA, ALBERT *with* LUISA. PLEKHANOV *speeds up still more, the dance grows still wilder and more elaborate. This goes on for some time, till the dancers are becoming visibly exhausted and rather unsteady with the champagne; they return gradually to the table and sit down, out of breath.* PLEKHANOV *stops playing, puts down his fiddle. A slight pause. Then* LUISA *grabs the other two bottles and gives them to* PLEKHANOV *and* BERGMAN, *who open them and pour more champagne.*)

ALBERT: Architects of the world, unite!

(*Hubbub.*)

ULCH: Special Secretaries of the world, depart for the next world!

(*Hubbub. They drain their glasses.* BERGMAN *and* PLEKHANOV *repour.*)

LUISA: Citizens of the world, love everybody in the world!

(*Hubbub.* PLEKHANOV *again seizes his fiddle and begins to play a wild csárdás.* LUISA *jumps on the table and begins to dance.* ULCH *collapses on the ground.* MACOURKOVA *takes him by the feet and, staggering, drags him towards the left rear door and out.* BERGMAN *gets up meanwhile, grabs the bottle and pours the rest of its contents over his head, after which he staggers to the staircase, falls against it and collapses to the floor.* RENATA, *who has drunk least, runs to him and eventually manages to get him to his feet, his arm round her neck, and helps him upstairs and goes out with him by the left door.* LUISA *continues to dance on the table, more wildly and provocatively, while* ALBERT *sits gazing up at her. There is a dissonant screech on the fiddle and* PLEKHANOV *stops playing, lets the fiddle fall from his hands, lets his head sink to his chest and immediately falls into a snoring sleep.* LUISA *stops dancing, laughs, sits on the table near* ALBERT *and turns to him.*)

ALBERT: You're wonderful . . .

(LUISA *begins to laugh. She takes the polystyrene model of the town with its castle, puts it on her head like an extraordinary hat, crosses her legs provocatively and assumes the pose of a courtesan.* ALBERT, *ignoring this, takes her hand and begins to speak rapidly, ignoring* PLEKHANOV's *snoring, which will accompany his whole speech.*)

Luisa – I know you'll probably make fun of me, but I'm absolutely serious about this: I love you! I love you madly. Of course it's ridiculous, it's stupid and mad. I know it's hopeless. I don't want anything from you, I've forbidden myself to want anything. It's entirely my problem, I've no right to bother you with it . . . It's enough for me just to see you now and then, during a meeting or at dinner . . . I respect your relationship with the chief, I'd give up my job rather than cause you the slightest trouble . . . This is the first and last time I shall mention it, I promise . . . Nothing like this has ever happened to me before . . . I don't understand it, I curse myself for it . . . but it's too strong for me . . . I probably wouldn't ever have mentioned it if it weren't for that wretched champagne . . . You're the sun in my life, all I want is the occasional ray falling on me from afar . . . that's all I need . . . I never dreamed love was like this, like falling over a precipice without the slightest control . . . My heart starts pounding whenever I see you, I'm behaving like a schoolboy, talking like a schoolboy . . . can't you help, make it stop, stamp on it, laugh at it, tell the chief, make it a house joke . . . I can't work, I see you all the time, everywhere, I've done no work for days now . . . Every night I have agonizing dreams about you . . . I hate myself that I can't control it, can't make it stop . . . I used to think I was a man, I was proud of my strong will, my self-control, suddenly I'm overwhelmed with feelings I don't understand . . . Not feelings, something else, something outside me, a demon possessing me . . . You're the one centre of my universe,

32

my axis, the source of my reality and meaning . . . I don't understand why God is testing me like this . . .

(*During* ALBERT'*s speech* LUISA *grows serious; she slowly removes her 'hat', tears come to her eyes, and she finally bursts into a loud sobbing.* ALBERT *stops.* LUISA *sits on the table, curled up in a ball, her hands covering her face.* ALBERT, *confused, gets up, not knowing what to do. Then he approaches* LUISA *cautiously and gently strokes her hair. She turns to him, still crying, pulls him to her and kisses him. Then she gently pushes him away. She controls her crying, dries her eyes, and tries to smile.*)

LUISA: I'm sorry. We're both idiots . . . drunken idiots . . .

ALBERT: Have I hurt you?

LUISA: Oh no . . .

ALBERT: Why are you crying?

LUISA: You wouldn't understand . . .

ALBERT: Please tell me.

LUISA: For myself.

(*She smiles sadly at him, then goes up to him and embraces him, and begins to kiss him gently.* ALBERT'*s eyes are closed; he stands there stupefied.* RENATA *enters by the left door. Seeing* LUISA *and* ALBERT *embracing, she stares at them in horror.* LUISA *gives* ALBERT *a final kiss and steps away from him, looking at him with a smile.* ALBERT'*s eyes remain closed.*)

(*Softly*) Albert . . .

(ALBERT *opens his eyes.*)

Enough now . . . I must be a sensible little girl. And you must be a sensible little boy. Promise me you'll be a sensible little boy?

(ALBERT *nods slightly.* RENATA *begins to sob quietly. Then the left rear door flies open and* ULCH *hurtles on, wearing only a shirt and underpants. His trousers and lab. coat come flying in after him.* ULCH *stops, looks round, sees* RENATA.)

ULCH: I have a sex drive too!

RENATA: (*Overcoming her sobbing*) I know you do . . .

(PLEKHANOV *suddenly wakes up with a start, obviously from*

some kind of awful dream. He looks ahead in alarm for a moment, then realizes where he is, picks up his fiddle and begins to play again the 'Blue Danube' waltz. As the lights dim the music grows fainter till it cannot be heard.)

ACT IV

The fiddle is heard playing 'Ochi Cherniya'. As the lights go up
PLEKHANOV *is seen playing, a white handkerchief round his head
like a bandage.* ALBERT *sits disconsolately nearby. A pause.*
RENATA *enters by the left door and stops on the landing, unnoticed
by the other two.*

RENATA: Excuse me, sir . . .
 (*Not hearing,* PLEKHANOV *plays on. A pause.*)
 Mr Plekhanov, sir . . .
 (*Still no response.*)
 Excuse me, sir!
 (PLEKHANOV *stops playing.*)
PLEKHANOV: Are you talking to me?
RENATA: The Project Director wondered if you had any more of
 your pills . . .
PLEKHANOV: My apologies, but I gave the last one to friend
 Ulch just now.
RENATA: I'll give him the message.
 (*She exits by the left door.* PLEKHANOV *puts down his fiddle.*)
PLEKHANOV: Albert, you really ought to have a little talk with
 Renata. Can't you see she's eating her heart out?
ALBERT: Over me?
PLEKHANOV: My head's splitting . . .
ALBERT: So's mine . . .
PLEKHANOV: I realize you have other things on your mind. I
 went through it myself twenty years ago. Even so . . .
ALBERT: I don't know what you went through twenty years ago,
 and you don't know what I'm going through now.
PLEKHANOV: But I do. We were at college together, I was in
 just the same boat as you are. Only of course she was
 twenty years younger then . . .
ALBERT: Are you talking about – ?
PLEKHANOV: Of course I am.
ALBERT: Has she told you anything?

35

PLEKHANOV: What about?

ALBERT: What happened yesterday.

PLEKHANOV: I don't know anything about yesterday; but I know what's going on with you.

ALBERT: Whatever you think you know, you don't understand.

PLEKHANOV: On the contrary, I'm the only one who does understand. I look at you and I see my younger self. That's why I'm worried about you.

ALBERT: Why?

PLEKHANOV: You don't know what you're getting into. I'm not in the habit of meddling with other people's affairs, but in this case . . .

ALBERT: Go on if you must.

PLEKHANOV: Your love appeals to her, you see, Albert, attracts her, excites her, that's why she can't put a stop to it. But at the same time she's incapable of taking that last wild step which would bring it to a head and save you. So she'll keep your love alive without ever fulfilling it. Sooner or later it'll drive you out of your mind, and there'll come some sort of casual tragedy. Believe me, I know what I'm talking about.

ALBERT: It happened to you? I mean . . .

PLEKHANOV: Never mind me, you're the one we're concerned with. Kill it, Albert, kill it now inside you, or you never will, unless you kill yourself, which I hope is not in your mind. After a certain stage, you know, some illnesses are incurable . . .

ALBERT: Love isn't an illness! Not love for her . . . Or do you think she's – a bad person?

PLEKHANOV: Bad? Not at all! That's the problem! That game she plays, you know, vague promises and partial repulses, those provocative hints at a longing, always in the end triumphantly controlled, that mixture of intimacy and inaccessibility – if that were just cold-blooded calculation or frivolous irresponsibility you'd see through it and cope with it. No, the devil of it is that she destroys not out of malice or simple-mindedness but out of her very nature . . . I apologize for the sermon. Put it down to that inner voice

36

you talked about not so long ago.

(*Pause.*)

ALBERT: It's odd.

PLEKHANOV: What is?

ALBERT: You try to warn me off her, and you've done the opposite: I'm beginning to understand that special sadness I see in her eyes . . .

PLEKHANOV: And that makes you feel even closer to her.

ALBERT: Yes.

PLEKHANOV: It intensifies your longing to help her.

ALBERT: Yes.

PLEKHANOV: You see that in this unfeeling world only your selfless love can protect her from the unhappiness she unconsciously creates for herself by unconsciously creating it in others . . .

ALBERT: Yes, yes.

PLEKHANOV: I was afraid that might happen. So I'd best do what I should have done in the first place: wish you good luck and hold my tongue.

(RENATA *enters by the left door with two cups of coffee on a tray, and goes slowly upstairs.* PLEKHANOV *nudges* ALBERT *to speak to her.*)

ALBERT: Renata . . .

(*She stops, then speaks without turning.*)

RENATA: Yes?

ALBERT: Do you have a few moments?

RENATA: I'm sorry but –

ALBERT: It's important.

RENATA: I have work to do.

ALBERT: We all have work to do. Please . . .

RENATA: I really can't just now . . .

(*She goes out quickly by the left upper door.* ALBERT *looks at* PLEKHANOV.)

PLEKHANOV: She's embarrassed. Run after her.

(*He gives* ALBERT *a little push, and* ALBERT *begins to go upstairs. But when he is only about three stairs up the left door opens and* LUISA *enters, a cup of coffee in each hand, leaving the*

37

door open. ALBERT *goes down, flustered, to make way for her.*)

ALBERT: (*Quietly*) Good morning . . .

LUISA: (*Cheerfully*) Good morning, Albert.

(She takes her cups to the table. PLEKHANOV *picks up his fiddle. Seeing him, the handkerchief round his head, she laughs.*)

You're not looking your usual self, Kuzma. Not like the Kuzma of old.

PLEKHANOV: (*Scowling*) I think I shall have a lie down . . .

(He shuffles out by the right rear door. LUISA *puts the coffee down, one for her, one for* BERGMAN, *sits and begins to stir hers; she glances at* ALBERT, *who still stands uneasily on the stairs. She smiles at him. A pause.*)

ALBERT: (*Quietly*) Forgive me . . .

LUISA: What for?

ALBERT: What happened yesterday.

LUISA: Don't be an idiot . . .

*(BERGMAN *enters by the left door, his head also bandaged with a handkerchief.*)

ALBERT: Good morning.

*(BERGMAN *gives a curt nod and goes to his place at the table. Forgetting that he was to go after* RENATA, ALBERT *wanders about indecisively for a moment or two, then:*)

I think I'll have a lie down too . . .

(And he goes out by the left rear door. BERGMAN, *sitting at his place, stirs his coffee. A pause.*)

BERGMAN: So how are you coping with the new – development?

LUISA: You can't expect me not to be touched.

BERGMAN: Touched, of course: love begets love.

LUISA: I said nothing about love.

BERGMAN: I'm sorry, let it remain unspoken . . . But you don't want to leave it there, surely?

LUISA: Maybe not, but I shall.

BERGMAN: Why is that?

LUISA: You wouldn't understand.

BERGMAN: No, of course I'm a man of stone as everyone knows. Feelings are your territory.

LUISA: It's your cynicism makes them my territory.

BERGMAN: Why will you leave it there?

38

LUISA: Because it's too serious to play with. I have no right. In
    case you haven't noticed, my territory includes
    responsibility from time to time.

BERGMAN: I'm afraid my brain is too coarse to figure out what
    can be so terribly serious about a sensitive and apparently
    innocent young man getting his head turned by an
    experienced woman in her forties. Still, I can be flattered: I
    suppose his falling for you is a kind of back-handed tribute
    to my good taste . . .

LUISA: Oh, he's only doing it to flatter you. Look, do you think
    we could try to be serious for a moment?

BERGMAN: I'm all for experiment.

LUISA: In the first place, I'd rather you didn't blame me for
    everything. I didn't set out to turn his head, I was as
    surprised as you were. Secondly, this is not a casual lust of
    the kind we're used to around here. There are depths we've
    forgotten about, if we ever knew them, and they're
    dangerous.

BERGMAN: For him, you mean?

LUISA: Perhaps for me too.

BERGMAN: One looks into the depths and wishes to fall . . .

LUISA: Well put.

BERGMAN: And is filled with terror.

LUISA: Quite so.

BERGMAN: So in fact you're afraid! You've looked into the
    depths . . .

LUISA: A glimpse.

BERGMAN: Not in my bed, I trust.

LUISA: If you're going to be tasteless we won't discuss it!

BERGMAN: Sorry. So how did you peer in?

LUISA: He told me terrifying things. Beautiful, but terrifying.

BERGMAN: For instance?

LUISA: That I'm the sun in his life, that he wants nothing more
    than for one of my rays to fall upon him from afar . . .

BERGMAN: What else?

LUISA: That his heart starts to pound the moment he sees
    me . . .

BERGMAN: Go on.

39

LUISA: He feels as if he's possessed by a demon. I'm the hub of his universe, the only source of its reality and meaning. (*The* SPECIAL SECRETARY *enters by the left door. He goes quickly upstairs, across the gallery and out through the right upper door.*)

BERGMAN: How strange.

LUISA: What is?

BERGMAN: That you, that well-known critic of the banal, should suddenly start to enjoy it.

LUISA: If you knew the smallest thing about love you'd know that the deeper the feeling, the harder it is to talk about; at its deepest, triteness is often all that works.

BERGMAN: I'll take your word for it. To get back to your famous sense of responsibility, does responsibility for me play any part in your considerations?

LUISA: Would you be upset if it didn't?

BERGMAN: I'm only interested.

LUISA: And I'm interested to know if you'd be upset.

BERGMAN: You needn't concern yourself with that any longer.

LUISA: What's that supposed to mean?

BERGMAN: Only that whatever happens I can't feel worse than I do now.
(*The* SPECIAL SECRETARY *enters by the right rear door and heads for the stairs.*)
Is anything wrong?

SPECIAL SECRETARY: Not at the moment.
(*He goes quickly upstairs and out by the left upper door.*)

LUISA: So here we go again.

BERGMAN: What do you mean?

LUISA: Turning the conversation back to your favourite subject. You're like a totally predictable character in a totally predictable play. Only since the last time I fell for your performance I've made a decision: not to buy another ticket. You can't put on your drama without an audience, can you? I wonder I didn't think of it long ago. I'm obviously one of those people who don't know what a play's about until they've seen it fifty times – Where are you going?

40

(BERGMAN *has stood up and is walking towards the stairs and up. He stops on the landing.*)

BERGMAN: Some plays, Luisa, you'll never understand until they're taken out of the repertory. As this one; you'll see. The performance is over, my love. Only this time the audience won't walk out of the play; the play will walk out of the audience. I hope you've enjoyed it . . .

(He turns and slowly, even ceremoniously, continues up the stairs. LUISA *watches for a moment without understanding; then she jumps to her feet.)*

LUISA: Zdenek!

BERGMAN: What do you want?

LUISA: Where the hell are you going?

BERGMAN: To the tower . . .

(He is already on the gallery and on his way to the right upper door. LUISA *runs up after him.)*

LUISA: Have you gone mad? Wait!

(She catches up with him and blocks his way. BERGMAN *pushes her away, but she grabs him and holds on tight. He tries to shake her off. There is a scuffle.)*

BERGMAN: Let go of me!

LUISA: Do you want me to make a scene? I'm going to scream . . .

BERGMAN: Do as you like. This is the end. Don't you understand? The end of everything! Will you let me go!

(The noise has attracted the others. ULCH *appears at the right upper door, a handkerchief round his head;* RENATA *at the left door;* ALBERT *at the left rear door; and at the right rear door,* PLEKHANOV *with his fiddle, his head still bound.)*

ULCH: I have a headache! What's going on?

LUISA: Stop him! Hang on to him!

(In front of the right upper door ULCH *struggles with* BERGMAN, *who is trying to escape; with their bound heads they struggle like Japanese wrestlers.* PLEKHANOV *puts down his fiddle and runs up to the gallery, followed by* ALBERT.*)*

BERGMAN: Ulch, I order you to let me go!

PLEKHANOV: What are we stopping him from doing?

LUISA: Don't ask questions, just stop him!

(PLEKHANOV, ULCH *and* ALBERT *hold on to* BERGMAN
firmly. BERGMAN *struggles for a while, then gives up.*)
BERGMAN: All right! Enough! I'll come.
(PLEKHANOV, ULCH *and* ALBERT *cautiously let him go.*
BERGMAN *goes slowly back along the gallery; as he passes*
LUISA *he hisses*:)
I'll still do it!
(*Just before* BERGMAN *reaches the left upper door the* SPECIAL
SECRETARY *comes out of it at speed and, taking no notice of
anyone, dashes downstairs, crosses the hall and out by the right
door, which he leaves open.* BERGMAN, *the others following,
comes quietly down the stairs. There is a pause as everyone
stands anxiously around the table.*)
PLEKHANOV: What's come over you, chief, for God's sake? And
now of all times, just when things are finally changing for
the better . . .
ULCH: Alcohol poisoning. Some people are worse with a
hangover than when they're drunk.
ALBERT: It's all my fault . . .
PLEKHANOV: Nonsense!
ALBERT: I know it is, don't try and comfort me.
LUISA: Oh, don't be an idiot.
(BERGMAN, *aware that everyone is staring at him, looks round
at them meaningfully. Slight pause.*)
BERGMAN: I'm not going to explain myself; you wouldn't
understand anyway. It's nothing to do with the project, still
less to do with you, Albert. If you must have a reason,
alcohol poisoning will do. But I'd prefer it if you'd forget
the whole sorry episode . . .
(*A dog starts barking wildly outside. Everyone looks curiously
towards the right door. The barking stops.* MACOURKOVA, *out
of breath, runs in by the left rear door. Soon afterwards, the*
SECOND INSPECTOR *enters by the right door, followed by the*
SPECIAL SECRETARY, *who closes the door behind him.*
BERGMAN, PLEKHANOV *and* ULCH *take off their
handkerchiefs and put them in their pockets. As everyone
watches them anxiously, the* SECOND INSPECTOR *and the*
SPECIAL SECRETARY *cross the stage pompously and climb the*

stairs, stopping in the middle of the gallery. The SECOND
INSPECTOR *takes a small sheet of paper from his pocket, clears
his throat and begins to read. The* SPECIAL SECRETARY *stands
just behind him, looking over his shoulder at the paper as he
reads.*)

SECOND INSPECTOR: (*Reading*) 'From time to time it becomes
necessary to bite on the apple no matter how sour; even,
sometimes, in the interests of the well-being of the people,
to take out the scalpel and excise the abscess. It hurts for a
while, but then the whole organism feels better. Some of
you may not find it easy at first to accept without question
or reservation what I am about to say. Finally, however,
you will reconcile yourselves to it, realizing that to use the
scalpel was the only way to save the patient.'

(MACOURKOVA *tiptoes out through the left rear door.*)

'My predecessor, whom you met here recently, was not a
bad fellow. Unfortunately, as you no doubt surmised
during your brief meeting, he fell short intellectually,
temperamentally and professionally of the demands of the
situation.'

(MACOURKOVA *returns by the left rear door with a glass of
water. She tiptoes across and up the stairs to put the glass on
the gallery railing in front of the* SECOND INSPECTOR, *then
goes quickly downstairs to join the others. The* SECOND
INSPECTOR *takes a drink and continues reading.*)

'A tragic figure, one could say: a simple man, a native of
this area, well intentioned and attuned to the mood of the
people but inexperienced in management, weak in public
relations and conceptually unsound. Thus it was that,
failing to sense the moment when freedom turns to
anarchy, unable in the hysterical atmosphere of unregulated
discussion to distinguish between those with honest ideas
and those without, he lost control of the situation. And so,
in his attempt to strengthen your autonomy as architects, to
listen to the voice of the people and so to improve the
quality of your work, he produced the direct opposite:
confusion spread and finally work here came to a complete
standstill . . .'

(*He pauses, looks down at the listeners and apparently begins to extemporize.*)

And if you don't work, what happens? I'll tell you, you don't eat! If you want to eat you've got to keep your nose to the grindstone! It's true for everyone! Even our grandmothers knew that. It's how things are! It's a fact of life! Anyone who doesn't understand that, what happens? He learns the hard way, through his teeth!

(*The* SPECIAL SECRETARY *gives the* SECOND INSPECTOR *an inconspicuous little nudge; the* SECOND INSPECTOR *understands at once and returns to the prepared text.*)

'Only after much urging from a number of honest people have I taken on the thankless task of restoring normality. But I shall not throw the baby out with the bathwater. On the contrary, I shall lift out the child, dry it off and nurse it to health that it may thrive and grow beautiful. But so that you don't think I'm a man of the old era, slavishly mouthing endless streams of meaningless verbiage, let me come straight to the point at issue: The decision to abandon the planned redevelopment project was rash, irresponsible, unprofessional and damaging, a stab to the heart of your mission, which is, to create better living conditions in a truly modern and conceptual manner. Preparations for the project will therefore continue as before, but with a new dynamism! Certain people will try to convince you that this is a return to old rightfully rejected methods. On the contrary! This is a radical renewal of the original intention, and a radical cleansing of former deformities calling for critical reform, as well as of all later excesses resulting from this criticism. I am confident that reason will triumph over emotion even among you, that even you will understand the urgent need for the necessary surgery, and that you will throw yourselves into the work with renewed vigour to make up for the unnecessary delay of the past weeks, which has caused such unease to the people down there. Good luck!'

(*He folds his piece of paper, puts it in his pocket, but feels it necessary to extemporize again.*)

Everyone's clamouring for a new toilet, tiles in the bathroom, white's not enough these days, they want black and God knows what! That's the way it is! That's the reality. Only that means someone's got to do what? Install it for them, yes! And before that, what? Design it, yes! That's how it always was and always will be, it's a fact of life, not just here, everywhere, anyone who doesn't understand that will get their – !

(*The* SPECIAL SECRETARY *leans forward to whisper something in his ear, pointing at his watch. The* SECOND INSPECTOR *nods, takes a drink of water, then together with the* SPECIAL SECRETARY *makes for the right door.*)

(*As he goes*) *Ciao* . . .

BERGMAN: *Ciao* . . .

(*The* SECOND INSPECTOR *and the* SPECIAL SECRETARY *go out by the right door, leaving the others motionless, staring dully after them. Long pause.*)

PLEKHANOV: So that's that.

(*He gives a little twang on his fiddle. A pause.*)

LUISA: We didn't enjoy that freedom for long.

(*A pause.*)

ULCH: I knew from the start it could only end one way. The last man was obviously a rank amateur . . .

(*A pause.*)

LUISA: He wasn't too clever, I agree. But what would he be doing in that job if he were?

(*A pause.*)

ULCH: You all laughed at me when I said we mustn't throw the baby out with the bathwater. And now you see what's happened.

(*A pause.*)

PLEKHANOV: Well, it was nice while it lasted.

LUISA: Like a dream.

PLEKHANOV: Better than a dream.

LUISA: At least we had a little dance.

PLEKHANOV: I just hope they're not tuning up for the big one.

LUISA: How is it we're so easily fooled?

PLEKHANOV: Only a corpse is never fooled.

(*After an embarrassed pause, they turn to look at* BERGMAN.)

BERGMAN: I think you're taking too gloomy a view, my friends. You know what I always say: what's done can't be undone, but every cloud has a silver lining. If you listened carefully you will have noticed that we're not required to revert *altogether* to the previous state of affairs. We've a little less room to manoeuvre, true, but we're used to that. We're going to have to bide our time for a while and keep our heads down. The first necessity in a new situation is to get one's proper bearings at the outset. We've lived through enough together – at least the older ones among us – to have the sense and experience to see this through as well. Personally I've never put much faith in great passions; easy come, easy go, I say. Less ambitious, more firmly based progress is of more value than high-flying manifestos. Manifestos don't build houses. We have to make careful assessments of what is practically feasible and what must be left temporarily in abeyance. We tried to run before we could walk, my friends, we made a number of high-sounding pronouncements with flowery words, forgetting that words are cheap. I include myself. One should not commit oneself to anything one is uncertain of being able to achieve. Feet on the ground, heads out of the clouds, we must cultivate the art of the possible. After all, architectural endeavour is never completely free, it exists in the social, economic and political context of the society it serves, a context it must respect. I'm not saying we shouldn't be bold. There are matters on which we must take a stance, points we must argue, that goes without question. All architects in all ages have had to decide when they should or must give way, and when they should stand firm. What is your opinion, Mrs Macourkova?

MACOURKOVA: Oh well, you know . . .

(*She shrugs her shoulders uncertainly.* ALBERT, *who has been listening carefully, suddenly speaks.*)

ALBERT: I'm getting out!

BERGMAN: I'm sorry?

ALBERT: I want to leave! This is making me sick!

46

BERGMAN: What is?

ALBERT: I don't understand what's going on! I don't understand anything.

BERGMAN: I can see this must have come as a shock to you, Albert, but a word of advice. Don't make rash decisions in the heat of the moment.

ALBERT: Do you remember yesterday? You were all trying to outdo each other! Never again would you betray your beliefs! Truth must destroy fear! Freedom must prevail over stupidity! And so on and so on, and then, suddenly, it's as if someone's waved a magic wand and you've been wiped clean, there's nothing left but how not to wet your pants as you run for cover! Is this normal? Does it go on everywhere? Are people just jellyfish? Am I mad, or are you?

(LUISA *goes up to* ALBERT *and pats him reassuringly.*)

LUISA: I understand your feelings, Albert, I really do. But try to understand us too. We shall need you now, more than ever. So promise me you'll be sensible.

ALBERT: I can't promise that, I'm sorry.

BERGMAN: As for those promises we made ourselves, Albert, they still stand. We simply have to find other ways of carrying them out. The fact is, in the excitement of the moment we let the idea of freedom go to our heads, unsurprisingly, and said some rather foolish things –

ALBERT: I didn't! I stand by everything I said!

BERGMAN: Albert, you're over-reacting. Calm down or you'll begin to make yourself ridiculous.

ALBERT: I don't care. I'd rather be ridiculous than lose my self-respect!

BERGMAN: I see. It's holier-than-thou you've decided to play, is it? The only one with clean hands? Well, please yourself. But I'm warning you, don't expect me to help next time you get yourself in a fix. If you want to put your head in a noose, go ahead and do it. But you're not going to put us in danger!

PLEKHANOV: Come, Zdenek, he's not putting us in danger.

BERGMAN: You know what he's trying to do? Prove himself a

real man! Well, as he knows himself, he's got a long way to go!

ALBERT: What do you mean by that?

BERGMAN: I don't know what kind of real man it is whose heart begins to pound every time he lays eyes on a sexually inviting middle-aged woman.

LUISA: (*Shrieks*) Bergman!

BERGMAN: I won't take lessons in self-respect from a retarded adolescent for whom a woman is the sun without whose rays he cannot live, nay verily the hub of his universe!

LUISA: You're revolting!

(LUISA *puts her head in her hands and bursts into tears.* ALBERT *looks despairingly at her, then at* BERGMAN, *then back at* LUISA. *He stands helplessly for a moment like a beaten dog, then suddenly runs upstairs as the* SPECIAL SECRETARY *enters by the left upper door and blocks his way. For a moment they look at each other silently.*)

SPECIAL SECRETARY: And where do you think you're going? (*A slight pause.*)

Well? Struck dumb? You had enough to say a moment ago; when you might have done well to listen to those wiser than you . . .

(ALBERT *pushes the* SPECIAL SECRETARY *aside and tries to pass him on the gallery. The* SPECIAL SECRETARY *seizes him expertly by the hand and twists it;* ALBERT *writhes in agony.*)

What do you say now? Are you going to be a sensible little boy?

ALBERT: What do you want?

(*The* SPECIAL SECRETARY *releases* ALBERT's *hand and smiles with satisfaction.* ALBERT *rubs his wrist.*)

SPECIAL SECRETARY: Well, I'm going to ask you a few questions.

ALBERT: Ask all you want, you won't get any answers.

SPECIAL SECRETARY: Oh, I shall. Come along.

(*The* SPECIAL SECRETARY *takes* ALBERT's *hand and drags him downstairs like a naughty schoolboy. The others watch this with amazement, making way for the* SPECIAL SECRETARY *and* ALBERT *as they go to the right rear door.*)

BERGMAN: May I ask the meaning of this?

SPECIAL SECRETARY: I'm afraid you'll have to do without this man's assistance for a while. He needs somewhere to think things over . . .

LUISA: Don't put him in the dungeon. Please, I beg. He's – he's ill, can't you see he's feverish!

SPECIAL SECRETARY: He'll soon cool down there . . .

MACOURKOVA: Secretary . . .

SPECIAL SECRETARY: What is it?

MACOURKOVA: Does your room need tidying? Shall I make your bed?

SPECIAL SECRETARY: No.

(*He opens the right rear door and pushes* ALBERT *through it.*)

RENATA: Albert!

(*The* SPECIAL SECRETARY *and* ALBERT, *in the doorway, look at* RENATA *in surprise.*)

Goodbye . . .

ALBERT: Goodbye, Renata.

(*The* SPECIAL SECRETARY *pushes* ALBERT *out firmly and also leaves.* RENATA *runs out by the left rear door, leaving it open.* MACOURKOVA, *also leaving, closes it behind herself. A long pregnant pause.*)

PLEKHANOV: The dance begins . . .

BERGMAN: I warned him.

ULCH: Much as I disagree with him, I feel a certain pity . . .

BERGMAN: It's a lesson he had to learn. Perhaps it'll teach him a little humility.

PLEKHANOV: You needn't have been so hard on him, you know . . .

BERGMAN: I'm only human, Kuzma!

PLEKHANOV: So is he.

(BERGMAN *goes up to* LUISA *and takes her hand.*)

BERGMAN: Luisa – I'm sorry I was indiscreet . . .

LUISA: Don't touch me!

(BERGMAN *moves away from her, embarrassed. A pause.*)

PLEKHANOV: No champagne today, I think . . .

(*Slight pause. Then something takes* LUISA's *attention. She*

49

walks around, sniffing. The others look at her,
uncomprehendingly. Slight pause.)
What's the matter?

LUISA: I smell gas . . .

(*The others begin to walk about sniffing.* LUISA *comes near the left rear door, sniffs for a while, then suddenly understands. She runs out through the left rear door, leaving it open. A moment later her horrified cry is heard.*)

(*Offstage*) Aahhh!

(*They all run towards the left rear door and go out through it, leaving it open.*)

(*Offstage*) Here, bring her here . . .

PLEKHANOV: (*Offstage*) Wait a minute – not like that – I'll do it myself . . .

LUISA: (*Offstage*) I should have known rightaway! Poor child!

BERGMAN: (*Offstage*) Well, this is all we needed!

PLEKHANOV: (*Offstage*) She'll come round in a minute . . . here . . . yes, that's the way . . .

LUISA: (*Offstage*) Brandy! Is there any brandy?

(*The voices grow quiet. A pause. The lights dim, in silence. Then we hear the fiddle offstage, playing a lyrical melody.*)

ACT V

LUISA *is listening closely as* PLEKHANOV *plays his fiddle. After a while he finishes the piece and puts the fiddle down.*

LUISA: *Do* I know that?
PLEKHANOV: Don't you?
LUISA: It sounds familiar . . .
PLEKHANOV: It should. I once played that to you every night at bedtime. One of those crazy outings of ours at the university.
LUISA: Of course! When we camped out in a hayloft!
PLEKHANOV: Exactly. Only there was no hay in it.
  (LUISA *muses for a moment. A pause.*)
LUISA: It's odd. I can remember it so clearly, but I don't feel part of it. As if it happened in a previous lifetime. Have I changed so much? It can't just be age, I'm not that old yet.
PLEKHANOV: To me you're always the same Luisa . . .
LUISA: Nonsense! Don't you remember how marvellously crazy I was? I grabbed at life then, every moment of it, no reservations, no second thoughts, no checking the exits just in case. Whatever caught my interest, I sacrificed everything for it, threw myself into it head first, blew through it like a tornado . . .
PLEKHANOV: Damaging a few items on the way.
LUISA: When did it all come to an end? And why? Look at me now: I've lost the knack of being happy. It's as if I'm in a train and hate the journey and haven't the nerve to jump out. I would have done then. What am I afraid of now?
PLEKHANOV: Remorse?
LUISA: On account of what?
PLEKHANOV: On account, perhaps, of the various items of goods you've damaged in your various jumps?
LUISA: I've never yet met an item of goods, as you put it, which wasn't damaged before I got there.
PLEKHANOV: All damaged goods? I suppose you're right. Only

dreams are pure and whole . . . Shall I tell you my attempt to cope with the problem? What they used to call fortitude. When I can no longer manage to be happy I try at least not to be unhappy; and when I can no longer spread more happiness than others I try at least not to spread more unhappiness.

LUISA: Do you apply that to your work as well?

PLEKHANOV: Oh yes, there as well. True, we'll spread misery among the people down there, but then indirectly they're responsible for spreading misery up here; architecture is well called the mirror of society. In other words we're applying the well-known Law of Universal Misery Exchange.

LUISA: Hardly something to be proud of.

PLEKHANOV: I'd say the only prideworthy item of goods up here is at present in the dungeon.

LUISA: Pride at second hand.

PLEKHANOV: Better than nothing.

(*A dog begins to bark wildy outside.* PLEKHANOV *and* LUISA *turn to look towards the right door. The barking stops and there is a knock on the door.*)

LUISA: Come in!

(*The* FIRST *and* SECOND WOMEN *enter by the right door. The* SECOND WOMAN *is black. Each carries a string bag containing three apples. They come down the stairs and stop.*)

FIRST WOMAN: Good afternoon.

LUISA: Good afternoon.

(*Slight pause.*)

FIRST WOMAN: I'd like to see the Project Director, please.

LUISA: I'll see if he's free.

FIRST WOMAN: Thank you.

(LUISA *goes upstairs towards the left door, but before she gets there* BERGMAN *comes out.*)

BERGMAN: What's going on?

LUISA: You've got visitors.

(BERGMAN *comes down the steps.* LUISA *hesitates, then also returns.* PLEKHANOV *picks up his fiddle and shuffles off, glances back curiously at the* WOMEN, *then goes out by the right rear door.*)

FIRST WOMAN: Good afternoon.

BERGMAN: Good afternoon.

(*He approaches the* WOMEN *and shakes their hands. Then he indicates that they are to sit down, and sits himself, but the* WOMEN *stay standing.* LUISA *stays to the left in the background. A slight pause.*)

What can I do for you?

FIRST WOMAN: We're the wives of the men who brought the petition . . .

BERGMAN: I remember them.

FIRST WOMAN: We want to ask if we can bring them this fruit.

BERGMAN: But they were released! Weren't they?

(*The* SPECIAL SECRETARY *enters by the left rear door and approaches.*)

SPECIAL SECRETARY: If you please.

(*He takes the bags from the* WOMEN *and tips the apples out on to the table. He shakes out the bags and examines them carefully, puts them aside and with a pen knife from his pocket he begins to cut the apples into pieces. A slight pause, as the others watch him intently.*)

FIRST WOMAN: Excuse me, they're not for you . . .

(*A slight pause as the* SPECIAL SECRETARY *continues.*)

Why are you cutting them up?

SPECIAL SECRETARY: Regulations. There could be a message hidden in one of them.

(*He has now cut up all the apples, which he carefully examines. Then he puts them back into the bags.*)

All clear.

FIRST WOMAN: So will you see that they get them?

SPECIAL SECRETARY: If they don't hinder the investigation they can have them at the proper time.

FIRST WOMAN: When's that?

SPECIAL SECRETARY: Fruit-transmission time.

FIRST WOMAN: When will that be?

SPECIAL SECRETARY: I don't carry all the details on me, you know.

FIRST WOMAN: Well, roughly . . .

SPECIAL SECRETARY: A month, say.

FIRST WOMAN: But they'll be rotten by then!

SPECIAL SECRETARY: I'm not responsible for nature's decaying processes.

(*He takes the bags and begins to climb the stairs. When he is about halfway the* SECOND WOMAN *speaks.*)

SECOND WOMAN: Sir . . .

SPECIAL SECRETARY: What's the matter?

SECOND WOMAN: We wanted to ask something else!

SPECIAL SECRETARY: Yes?

SECOND WOMAN: Why are they back in there after you let them out?

SPECIAL SECRETARY: There's reason to suspect that they are in possession of the facts.

SECOND WOMAN: What facts?

SPECIAL SECRETARY: The real intention of the petition.

SECOND WOMAN: But its real intention was what was written on it.

SPECIAL SECRETARY: So we thought until recently.

SECOND WOMAN: What do you think now?

SPECIAL SECRETARY: Things are surfacing you'd hardly believe.

SECOND WOMAN: What things? We've a right to know.

SPECIAL SECRETARY: You haven't, but I'll tell you anyway. We have evidence to show this was not an innocent petition on behalf of the people, obviously no one would object to that, but a well-timed and carefully engineered signal for the unleashing of mass hysteria, of which you know the tragic consequences. You must see that to avoid such a thing ever happening again we must find the truth and learn from it. Do you have any children?

SECOND WOMAN: Eight.

SPECIAL SECRETARY: There you are then!

(*He quickly crosses the gallery and goes out by the right upper door. A tense pause. Then* LUISA, *after making sure the* SPECIAL SECRETARY *is gone, glances at all the doors then takes out her purse, takes a banknote from it and tries to push it*

into the hands of first the SECOND *then the* FIRST WOMAN.
The WOMEN *want to refuse it.*)

SECOND WOMAN: No, really, no . . .

FIRST WOMAN: It's very nice of you but we can't –

LUISA: Please.

*(There is a confused battle with the note, during which it falls
to the floor.* LUISA *and the* FIRST WOMAN *bend together to
pick it up, bumping their heads. Finally* LUISA *succeeds in
stuffing the note into the* SECOND WOMAN's *blouse.*)

SECOND WOMAN: Well, thank you –

FIRST WOMAN: Goodbye . . .

(They exit in embarrassment by the right door. LUISA *sighs and
wipes her forehead.*)

BERGMAN: Do you know what repercussions that could have?
You must be mad.

LUISA: Don't talk to me! You're despicable . . .

(She begins to climb the stairs, watched by BERGMAN.)

BERGMAN: Luisa!

*(*LUISA *ignores him. A slight pause, then* BERGMAN *runs after
her, catches her and takes her hand.* LUISA *tries to get away.*)

LUISA: Let go! Or I'll start screaming!

BERGMAN: Luisa, you've already behaved stupidly, if you start
a scene you'll only make it worse.

LUISA: Leave me alone, you disgust me.

BERGMAN: What have I done?

LUISA: You ask that after yesterday?

BERGMAN: Oh, that . . .

LUISA: Yes, that. Can you imagine what a shock it must have
been for him? To have you repeating his words in front of
everybody? I knew you were unfeeling, but I never thought
you'd stoop so low. He trusted me, only me. Now his
whole world has collapsed. How do you think he feels
down there?

BERGMAN: All right, it was stupid of me. I got carried away.
It's my nerves, things get on top of me. You've got to
remember what I'd just been through.

LUISA: You?

BERGMAN: The moat! I was within an ace of it!

LUISA: You weren't within an ace of anything.

BERGMAN: So why did you make such a fuss about it?

LUISA: Because I'm an idiot. You put on your melodrama and I fall for it.

BERGMAN: Don't worry, I shan't mention it again; the play is over. I'll do it secretly when you least expect it, maybe at night –

LUISA: If the play were really over you wouldn't be telling me that now.

BERGMAN: They'll find me there one morning. There'll be an argument over who should break the news to you. Plekhanov will do it. You'll cry for a while, reproach yourself for not taking me seriously; remember happier times like the time we sat all night on the pier talking about our lives and drinking muscatel wine – seven years ago was it? – making love as the sun came up and rolling into the sea . . . Or at that international post-modern architecture conference, when we walked through the palm groves night after night long after everyone else had gone . . . Till you have to force yourself to stop thinking about it . . . You'll cry through the funeral, and then – by the way, will you ask Plekhanov to play that song, what's it called? The sad one. Special request . . . Then in time life will return to normal, more or less. Albert will come out of the dungeon and you'll take long nostalgic walks together, talking about me; he'll hardly dare touch you, but his devotion will move you the more. Gradually you'll transfer your feeling from the dead man who no longer needs it to the living one; you'll say to yourself: he always wanted peace, eternal, absolute, definitive peace and now he's got it . . . And if Albert's love endures, which I'm sure it will, he's not superficial, if I seemed to be cynical about his feelings it was only I was so moved . . . even aroused, I'll admit it – to see the excitement in your eyes, your cheeks flushing as you thought of the depths of his emotion, depths a clod like me could never plumb – so if his love endures and his love enters into your soul, becoming the one certainty in your life – then all at once it will happen – you yourselves won't

56

even know how – all at once it will seem so obvious, so simple, so natural and so pure . . . Then that glorious stage of getting to know each other more and more profoundly – that enchantment with each special little feature you discover on each other, a freckle on the underbelly, a cleft ear-lobe, his particular way of shaking all over as he brushes his teeth, the double nail on his foot – and the time will come when you'll forget me completely, I shall evaporate like steam together with all the happy, sad, absurd experiences we went through together, disappear into some kind of black hole somewhere far away in the universe, and that will be my second death, the truly final and truly definitive one . . .

(LUISA, *overcome with emotion, falls to* BERGMAN'*s feet, embraces them, puts her head in his lap and begins to sob loudly.* BERGMAN *caresses her tenderly, then he carefully lifts her and kisses her tear-stained eyes. They smile at each other.* BERGMAN *gets up, takes* LUISA *by the hand.*)

Let's go . . .

LUISA: Where?

BERGMAN: You know.

LUISA: Now?

BERGMAN: Why not?

(*He takes* LUISA'*s hand and leads here towards the stairs and up. As they are about to go out through the left door a dog begins to bark wildly outside. At this moment the* SPECIAL SECRETARY *bursts in by the right upper door, crosses the gallery and comes down the stairs at a run.* BERGMAN *and* LUISA *look at him in surprise. He sees them.*)

SPECIAL SECRETARY: Call everyone together!

(*He goes quickly to the right door and out, leaving it open.* ULCH *appears at the right upper door,* PLEKHANOV *with his fiddle at the right rear door; both watch what is going on curiously, until the barking subsides.*)

(*Offstage*) Hallo!

SECOND INSPECTOR: (*Offstage*) Ciao! Are they ready for me, Mishak?

SPECIAL SECRETARY: (*Offstage*) All ready.

(BERGMAN, LUISA *and* ULCH *come downstairs,* PLEKHANOV *puts his fiddle away. They all look towards the right door.* MACOURKOVA, *panting, runs in by the left rear door. After a moment the* SECOND INSPECTOR *enters by the right door, followed by the* SPECIAL SECRETARY, *who closes the door behind him. They stop on the steps. The* SECOND INSPECTOR *looks at the confused faces with a smile.*)

SECOND INSPECTOR: *Ciao!*

BERGMAN: (*Uncertainly*) *Ciao* . . .

SECOND INSPECTOR: Sit down.

(*They all sit down with embarrassment round the table. The* SECOND INSPECTOR *sits on the steps by the right door, the* SPECIAL SECRETARY *beside him. The* SECOND INSPECTOR *takes out a sheet of paper, unfolds it, clears his throat and begins to read. The* SPECIAL SECRETARY *peers over his shoulder at the paper.*)

'I'm sure you'll agree that we've come a long way. We have purged the forward-looking concepts contained within the previous criticism of early deformation of our strategy of housing modernization on which the present project is based, of their later backward-looking disinterpretations, thus allowing us to purge the strategy itself of its former deformations. This was not easy; but we can proudly claim success. Nevertheless we must not rest on our laurels. On the contrary: the success of our achievements obliges us to admit openly that the path we have set will achieve its goal only when we have rolled away the boulder of stagnation that time has put in its way. . .'

(*He interrupts his reading to extemporize.*)

In other words, time marches on! Not only here, the world over! And if anyone here thinks otherwise – !

(*The* SPECIAL SECRETARY *gives him an inconspicuous nudge. He understands, and returns to the paper.*)

'This, of course, needs the co-operation of all concerned. It has been decided therefore that the development project must harmonize with the new degree of understanding of our new-found but temporarily frozen potentialities which once released must be thrown with all urgency into primal dialogue as to the optimal alternatives regarding our future evolution. This, it goes without saying, demands that we rid ourselves of fear and conformism, overcome indolence and indifference, and look truth courageously in the eye, fearlessly casting outdated ways of thought into the dustbin and searching freely for new and unconventional approaches. In this endeavour you have my full support!'

(*He folds up his paper, puts it in his pocket and gets up, as does the* SPECIAL SECRETARY. *The* SECOND INSPECTOR, *however, feels called on to extemporize again.*)

Nothing works without freedom, even my grandmother knew that, and Mishak's here, yours too, everyone's, black or white! It's a fact of life, whether you like it or not, so get your fingers out, otherwise – !

(*The* SPECIAL SECRETARY *leans over to whisper something in his ear, pointing to his watch. The* SECOND INSPECTOR *nods.*)

MACOURKOVA: Look after yourself, Inspector! We need you!

(*The* SECOND INSPECTOR *goes up to* MACOURKOVA, *puts a hand on her shoulder and looks into her eyes.*)

SECOND INSPECTOR: Don't worry. *Ciao!*

MACOURKOVA: *Ciao!*

(*The* SECOND INSPECTOR *and the* SPECIAL SECRETARY *go out by the right door. A slight pause.* LUISA *whispers something into* MACOURKOVA'*s ear,* MACOURKOVA *nods, and they both go out by the left rear door. The others take their usual places at the table. A long, oppressive pause.*)

PLEKHANOV: Did you know we have a stork nesting on the tower?

ULCH: Is that good luck or bad luck?

PLEKHANOV: It depends how you look at it . . .

(*A long, oppressive pause.*)

BERGMAN: While we're on the subject, there's a hole in the vegetable garden fence. The rabbits are eating the cabbages.

ULCH: I noticed that. I've been meaning to repair it but things come up . . .

PLEKHANOV: I'll fix it tomorrow . . .

(*A long oppressive pause.*)

ULCH: The magnolias in the park are in bloom already.

PLEKHANOV: Except for two; a later variety.

(*Pause.* LUISA *and* MACOURKOVA *come in by the left rear door*, LUISA *carrying a tray with five plates of food and cutlery*, MACOURKOVA *a tray with a jug of beer and five glasses. They set everything out on the table, put the trays down and take their seats. Pause. Everyone looks at* BERGMAN, *whose mind is elsewhere. He comes to himself.*)

BERGMAN: *Bon appetit*!

(*They all begin to eat. A long oppressive pause.*)

PLEKHANOV: How's Renata?

LUISA: A bit weak; but she'll probably get up tomorrow.

(*A long oppressive pause.*)

BERGMAN: Is there mint in this?

LUISA: I did put some in. I found some growing in the garden.

BERGMAN: Where in the garden?

LUISA: Right at the back, by the septic tank.

(*A long oppressive pause.*)

ULCH: When I was a lad I used to play the violin. You must lend me yours sometime, Plekhanov.

PLEKHANOV: Of course. Gladly . . .

(*Pause. The* SPECIAL SECRETARY *comes in by the right rear door.*)

SPECIAL SECRETARY: How's the discussion coming along? What conclusions have you reached?

(*An embarrassed pause.*)

BERGMAN: Nothing of substance yet . . .

SPECIAL SECRETARY: Keep at it. Don't be afraid to say what you think!

(*He goes out by the left rear door. A long oppressive pause.*)

PLEKHANOV: I can't wait to get to bed today . . .

BERGMAN: I feel that every day.

(*A long oppressive pause.*)

ULCH: Anyway, it was him she did it for!

PLEKHANOV: Not for you, certainly.

LUISA: She's all right, that's the main thing.

(*A long oppressive pause.*)

BERGMAN: What about tomorrow? Have you worked anything out?

LUISA: I found some mince. So I'll probably make a meat loaf.

ULCH: I'm fond of meat loaf. But only if there's cabbage in it.

LUISA: I don't know if we have any cabbage.

ULCH: No cabbage?

LUISA: The rabbits, you see.

(*Pause. The* SPECIAL SECRETARY *enters by the left upper door and comes down the steps.*)

SPECIAL SECRETARY: Well? Are you full of ideas?

(*Embarrassed pause.*)

BERGMAN: Actually the morning is our time for new ideas . . .

SPECIAL SECRETARY: I wouldn't put it off too long. The situation is grave, the sooner we come up with something new the better.

(*He goes towards the right rear door.*)

LUISA: Secretary . . .

SPECIAL SECRETARY: What's the matter?

LUISA: Don't you think Albert could be let out now?

SPECIAL SECRETARY: I'll ask.

(*He goes out by the right rear door. Pause.*)

BERGMAN: Do you think that was wise?

LUISA: It would have carried more weight if you'd said it.

BERGMAN: I was going to, of course. At the right moment. When I was alone with him or . . .

PLEKHANOV: I think I've worked out where the secret passage went.

ULCH: If there ever was one.

PLEKHANOV: There are several mentions in the archives.

ULCH: For what they're worth.

PLEKHANOV: At a certain spot on the rear wall of that little chamber to the right of the deepest of the cellars, directly beneath the dungeon, there are definite signs of new brickwork . . .

(*A pause. Then the* SPECIAL SECRETARY *and* ALBERT *enter by the right rear door.* ALBERT *looks ill, his face drawn.*)

SPECIAL SECRETARY: So, here he is.

LUISA: Albert!

(*The* SPECIAL SECRETARY *goes out by the left rear door.*
LUISA *jumps up, rushes over to* ALBERT *and embraces him.*
But ALBERT *shows no reaction.* LUISA *steps back in surprise.*
PLEKHANOV *also gets up, goes to* ALBERT *and gives him a*
friendly slap on the back. ALBERT *shows no reaction.*
PLEKHANOV, *puzzled, goes back to his place in*
embarrassment. Pause.)

BERGMAN: Sit down, everyone, please.

(ALBERT *goes to his place mechanically and sits. A pause.*)

ULCH: Bad, was it?

(ALBERT *shrugs his shoulders. A pause.*)

LUISA: Why don't you say something? Aren't you glad to be
out?

(ALBERT *shrugs his shoulders. A pause.*)

BERGMAN: He's a little confused. Anyone would be.

ULCH: Give him a day or two, he'll be back to normal.

LUISA: Aren't you hungry?

(ALBERT *shakes his head. A pause.*)

ULCH: Did you hear about Renata?

(ALBERT *shakes his head. A pause.*)

LUISA: She'll be up and about tomorrow. It wasn't your fault.
You're not blaming yourself, are you?

(ALBERT *shakes his head. A pause.*)

PLEKHANOV: What about the other two? Have they let them
out?

(ALBERT *shakes his head. A pause.*)

LUISA: But they gave them the apples at least?

(ALBERT *shakes his head. A pause.*)

BERGMAN: The main thing now is to get a good rest. Get your
thoughts together . . . stabilize your feelings . . . get your
bearings *vis-à-vis* the present situation . . .

(*Slight pause. Then* ALBERT *rises slowly and as if*
sleepwalking walks towards the stairs. The others watch him as
he mounts the stairs, crosses the gallery and goes out by the right
upper door.)

I didn't expect him to take it so hard . . .

ULCH: It's really done him in.

LUISA: He's sensitive. God knows what they did to him . . .

BERGMAN: Maybe he'll be more careful from now on.
　　(*Slight pause. Then* PLEKHANOV, *deep in thought, rises and goes towards the stairs.*)
LUISA: Kuzma?
　　(PLEKHANOV *takes no notice.*)
　　Are you afraid he might . . .?
　　(PLEKHANOV, *ignoring her, goes up the stairs, crosses the gallery and out by the right upper door. The* SPECIAL SECRETARY *comes in by the left upper door, comes downstairs to the landing and stops.*)
SPECIAL SECRETARY: I'm looking forward to the morning!
　　(*They look at him blankly.*)
　　Your ideas. We need to learn from you, you know.
MACOURKOVA: Won't you join us in our deliberations, Secretary, I'm sure we should benefit!
SPECIAL SECRETARY: I'm afraid I have studies of my own.
　　(*He goes out by the left door. A very long oppressive pause. Then suddenly crashing sounds are heard outside as of something heavy falling, crashing into obstacles on the way, followed by a very loud dull thud, as if something had hit the ground from a great height. There is total silence for a moment; they look at one another, transfixed.*)
LUISA: Oh, my God!
　　(*At that moment they all understand what has happened. They run to the rear doors.* BERGMAN *and* LUISA *go out by the left rear door, and* ULCH *and* MACOURKOVA *by the right rear door; both doors are left open. The stage is empty, there is silence. Then* ULCH *and* MACOURKOVA *come in by the left rear door and at the same time* BERGMAN *and* LUISA *by the right rear door. They walk to the middle of the room, frowning, at a solemn, slow pace as if walking behind the coffin at a funeral. They form a half-circle round the table. The* SPECIAL SECRETARY *enters by the left door and stands on the landing.* BERGMAN *slowly crosses to the stairs, climbs them to the landing, steps up to the balustrade and turns to the others as if to give a funeral oration. The* SPECIAL SECRETARY *stands behind him.*)
BERGMAN: Needless to say, we are all deeply affected by what

has happened. Not only because of the loss of a much-loved colleague and friend, but because we all carry a share of guilt in regard to his death. We are all responsible for the sad shape our world is in, which has hounded a sensitive man beyond the limits of endurance. We're callous, indolent, indifferent, deaf to the voices of those near and dear to us and blind to their pain. But this bitter consciousness of our complicity has a positive side: we alone, it tells us, can ensure that the death of our friend was not in vain. We alone can give it sense by seeing it as an appeal to us to strive to make a more bearable and more habitable world. Let us therefore promise ourselves at this difficult time that we will never again allow human apathy to rule and destroy. Let us vow never again to connive in the 'redevelopment' of the souls of ourselves or others. Our mission is not to dance to the frivolous beat of an incompetent conductor, but to hold fast to the truth we have found, and dedicate ourselves to the work we have begun. Only thus shall we be true to the moral legacy of this terrible and unexpected death. Only thus can we respond with dignity to the warning voice which calls even now from the depths of the castle moat. Only thus can we show that we hear that voice of reproach and that its message has been understood.

(BERGMAN *comes down the stairs, takes* PLEKHANOV'*s fiddle, places it ceremoniously on the table and sits behind it.*)

(*To the fiddle*) We promise you, Kuzma Plekhanov, that we shall not forget!

(*He takes a flower from his breast pocket and places it on the fiddle, assuming a pious pose. The left and right upper doors open simultaneously.* RENATA, *in a nightgown, enters by the left,* ALBERT *by the right upper door. Both stop on the landing. A slight pause.*)

ALBERT: Did you know we have a stork nesting on the tower?
RENATA: I have a sex drive too!

(*A slight pause. Then* LUISA *begins to sob loudly; she goes to the table still sobbing and hysterically grabs the model of the castle with both hands, raises it above her head and with a*

64

wild swing down jams it on BERGMAN's *head so forcefully that his entire face disappears inside.* BERGMAN *continues to stand immobile as if nothing has happened. The others turn to the audience and stare fixedly into the eyes of individual members of it. The song 'Ochi Cherniya' is heard softly, played by a full orchestra. As the stage darkens, the sound grows louder and the house lights begin to brighten. When the stage is dark the music reaches a crescendo, playing at almost deafening volume. Then it suddenly stops; there are several seconds of silence; then music is heard again, but this time, at a reasonable level, Karajan's recording of Strauss's 'Blue Danube' waltz, which will continue until the auditorium is completely empty.)*

FABER DRAMA

W. H. AUDEN
ALAN AYCKBOURN
PETER BARNES
SAMUEL BECKETT
ALAN BENNETT
STEVEN BERKOFF
ALAN BLEASDALE
ANNE DEVLIN
T. S. ELIOT
BRIAN FRIEL
ATHOL FUGARD
TREVOR GRIFFITHS
CHRISTOPHER HAMPTON
DAVID HARE
TONY HARRISON
VÁCLAV HAVEL
SHARMAN MACDONALD
FRANK McGUINNESS
RICHARD NELSON
JOHN OSBORNE
HAROLD PINTER
DENNIS POTTER
SAM SHEPARD
TOM STOPPARD
TIMBERLAKE WERTENBAKER
NIGEL WILLIAMS